ELVIS SPEAKS FROM THE BEYOND
and Other Celebrity Ghost Stories

ELVIS SPEAKS FROM THE BEYOND

and Other Celebrity Ghost Stories

HANS HOLZER

GRAMERCY BOOKS
NEW YORK

This 1999 edition is published by Gramercy Books,™
an imprint of Random House Value Publishing, Inc.,
201 East 50th Street, New York, New York 10022.

Gramercy Books™ and design are trademarks of
Random House Value Publishing, Inc.

Random House
New York • Toronto • London • Sydney • Auckland
http://www.randomhouse.com/

Printed and bound in the United States of America

A CIP catalog record for this book is available from the Library of Congress.

Elvis Speaks from the Beyond and Other Celebrity Ghost Stories /
by Hans Holzer
ISBN 0-517-20716-8

8 7 6 5 4 3 2 1

It is such a short distance
from here to there.
                 —Eileen Garrett

Contents

Foreword

People who have psychic experiences, especially those who communicate with or have visions of dead relatives or friends, are often reluctant to talk about them out of fear of being ridiculed. While this holds true for many in the ordinary walks of life, it most certainly holds true for those who are in the public eye. Politicians and celebrities are particularly careful about telling the world—and the press —about such encounters.

I am therefore pleased to include in this book true experiences by people who were not reluctant to own up to their encounters with the world beyond. This is particularly gratifying for me, as I believe that the more the famous people of this world report their psychic encounters, the more legitimate this subject will become.

Life is continual: it does not end at death's door. The true stories presented here bear witness to it. The cases reported herein are in no way fictional. The people who have had these experiences are rational, hard-working individuals.

Celebrity ghosts are no different from the ghosts of the unknown, but the interest in them, naturally, is at least as great as the fascination with the celebrity involved. *Elvis Speaks from the Beyond and Other Celebrity Ghost Stories* offers a unique perspective for anyone curious about what happens to the rich and famous in the next world.

Hans Holzer, Ph.D.

Elvis Speaks *from the Beyond*

Elvis Presley died on August 16, 1977, at the age of forty-two, but today he is more alive than ever. There are persistent reports of people having seen Elvis walking out of a drugstore, driving a flashy car, or waving hello, but he never seems to stand still long enough to be identified positively as the King of Rock 'n' Roll—because it isn't him, really. Look-alikes galore are populating second-class nightclubs, and the sales of Elvis costumes and memorabilia are brisker than ever. And this does not even account for the souvenirs sold at Graceland, his old home, where the faithful go to bask in his memory, especially on the anniversary of his passing.

So if Elvis is really, really dead and gone . . . where exactly, ah, is he? And how is he doing? We have lots of claims by people who say they have recently heard from the King, that is, the-King-who-is-over-there. Some of these claims of contact come from psychics and would-be psychics who in their entire life never met with Elvis, despite his interest in the paranormal, but who quickly discovered their own celebrity status when newspaper reporters were eager to quote them. This all started almost immediately after Elvis's untimely death. By 1979, there was a veritable avalanche of claims.

In April 1979, Carmen Rogers held a seance during which Elvis allegedly told her what he wanted done about his fortune, his children, and his relatives. It was a seance held for the benefit of a reporter, though none of the information was exactly unknown.

A tourist named Lorraine Hartz claims to have seen Elvis's spirit while visiting Graceland. Others have felt his presence in the Graceland house, which of course may only be a psychic imprint from the past. Medium Lou Wright has often claimed contact with the King after his passing, but without, however, giving the kind of hard evidence a trained parapsychologist such as myself would find acceptable. Still, according to Elvis sidekick Charlie Hodge, Elvis did know Lou Wright personally in his lifetime. Even in far-away Australia, "Mr. John," an artist-turned-psychic some years ago, could not resist the temptation to make contact with Elvis by holding what his newspaper sponsors called "the seance of the century." In 1982, Violet Rosenberg, a London psychic, told audiences at a psychic fair that Elvis would "return to London" within a month. (By then the psychic fair would be over.)

But the pronouncement of this lady prompted another young woman, named Joy Hatfield, to contact me. Yes, she told me, Elvis did attend that convention, but he did not like the setup, so he didn't appear. Joy then sent me pages and pages of claims and also some interesting psychic photos, and eventually decided to write a book about her life (or afterlife) with Elvis.

"Elvis first contacted me on the day he was buried," she explained to me. This led to a string of visitations by the late singer, with whom she identified more and more as time went on. She said that she and Elvis were together in another lifetime.

In New England, there is a woman named Marcia Jones, who contacted me in May of 1979 because Elvis was creating problems in her life by singing "through" her. For proof, she sent me a tape of some of Elvis's favorite songs. Marcia Jones was sincere—she even wanted the Presley family to know. When I expressed the desire to have some more solid evidence, I received a handwritten note from her, asking me to show "these songs to Daddy and family . . . Marcia is the only one on earth closest to my heart . . . God said I would live through her." It was signed "Elvis Presley." Her "involvement" with Elvis caused such a stir with her family and friends that ultimately I had to tell her that the "automatic writing" of the note was not at all like Presley's and that the songs on the tape were not likely to have been Elvis's choice. For a while I heard nothing further from her, but in May of 1982, she contacted me again. She still "loved" Elvis, but it wasn't easy for her; she even confronted her Elvis with reports of his talking to other women(!) from Over There, but he assured her, she says, that these claims were false and that he was only with her. I have heard nothing from Marcia since then.

What makes these people reach out to Elvis and become convinced he is in contact with them? Being an intimate of a celebrity, even a dead one, takes you out of your ordinary environment—and dead celebrities can't be checked out.

With all this in mind, I was less than enthusiastic when a close friend of mine wanted me to talk to a woman from New Jersey, whose daughter had apparently had a visit from Elvis. But he insisted, and eventually I gave in and received the woman, expecting another would-be Elvis contactee. Instead, it turned into a real-life detective story, and for the first time, I had proof that Elvis was, in fact, alive and well—Over There.

Dorothy Sherry came to see me at my study in Manhattan. Haltingly, she explained that she had on occasion been psychic, such as the time when she "saw" a vision of an extremely fat man with a cigar in his mouth, a very red face, and a hat perched on the back of his head. When she mentioned it to her mother, her mother took out the family album and showed her, for the first time, a picture of her long-dead uncle!

But the thing that really shook her happened one day early in January 1978 (she didn't know the exact date because she hadn't bothered to keep notes), when the name of Elvis Presley suddenly burst into her mind, and just as quickly, he appeared to her.

"I was fully awake at the time," Dorothy explained, "sitting on my couch, with all the lights on. He wore a white shirt open at the neck, with folded-up cuffs, and he held out his hand to me, saying, 'You can come with me now.' "

It appears that Dorothy obeyed and held out her hand. Only it wasn't her physical hand, which stayed with her body on the couch, but the hand of her spirit. Elvis was taking her on an astral flight, which parapsychologists call an out-of-the-body experience, the first of many such flights she was to undertake in the months to come.

When I realized who the spirit communicator was, I began to question Dorothy severely. I spoke to her mother and to our mutual friend—she was telling the truth. There was no unusual interest in either Presley or rock 'n' roll music. The contact had come spontaneously, out of the blue as it were.

"It was around eleven at night. My husband was already asleep. I took Elvis's hand, and as I turned around I looked back at myself sitting on the couch. Then we went through a sort of tube or tunnel, with bright lights on the other end. Next, we ended up in a beautiful field covered with grass and beautiful flowers."

"Didn't it seem strange that a famous singer like Elvis Presley should choose to make contact with you?" I inquired.

"As a matter of fact that was the first thing I asked him. How come *me?* We talked for over four hours that night. He said he had known me in a previous life, and that I had been his wife. I said I found that extremely hard to believe. But he assured me it was so. Then he talked about his daughter, his ex-wife, and some of the things he had done for which he was now sorry, especially the way he died."

"How did you get back?"

"He walked me back, kissed me on the cheek, and the next thing I know, I'm back on my couch."

Elvis met her again the night after and this time his mother was with him. Evidently the mother disapproved of Dorothy, so Dorothy got scared and Elvis didn't return for two weeks. But Dorothy still couldn't get used to the idea that it was really him, and she began to worry about her sanity. Her mother had read some of my books and was wondering how she could get in touch with me for advice. Meanwhile, Dorothy went astral traveling with Elvis practically night after night. Apparently, he took her to visit places that had meant something to him in his life.

"I've been taken to Las Vegas, in his dressing room at the Hilton Hotel, in the penthouse, and even on the stage. I've been to the house he had when he died, and another place, a long, beautiful ranch house, and he seems to be looking for something when we get there."

"Can you actually feel him?"

"Oh yes, I can feel his shirt, his face, and his hands . . . they're callused and he bites his fingernails."

Dorothy, though calmer now, still couldn't get it through her head that she was taking astral flights with the late Elvis Presley. What was he doing with a simple housewife? Again and again, Presley talked of their previous life together and his realization that he would be with her again in a future lifetime.

Elvis, according to Dorothy, explained he was happy to be reunited with his mother, dead many years. Though he seemed upset concerning his daughter on earth, he felt serene in his new environment.

"If it seems brighter here, it is because God is all around us. The higher you go, the brighter it gets as you get closer to God," Dorothy quotes Elvis as telling her.

But Dorothy still wouldn't accept the situation, so on one astral flight, Elvis arranged for Dorothy's dead grandmother to speak to her.

"I didn't expect to see her," Dorothy explained, "I was with Elvis, and we were walking down this dirt road, over there, and suddenly there she was. 'How is he treating you?' my grandmother asks me, and well, I like to kid, so I say, 'He's doing alright.' With that she turns on him and screams, 'You got special permission for this, you're supposed to help my granddaughter, I'm not here anymore and I'm depending on you!'"

"How did you feel about this?"

"I began to tell myself, well, this must be happening, I couldn't make it all up! I don't have that kind of imagination."

Dorothy couldn't be more right. She was a pleasant, average housewife, in her early thirties, with two growing kids, a husband who won't have any truck with "the supernatural," and not the sort of person who would go out of her way to get attention or cause waves.

She decided she would confide in her mother, who immediately suggested that I be contacted. Her mother understood, for she too had had occasional ESP experiences and took Dorothy at her word, especially since she was with her daughter on several occasions when Elvis appeared. To Dorothy, he was a three-dimensional man, but to her mother "a shadow." Then "the shadow" spoke, and Dorothy's mother clearly heard him say to her, "Don't worry, I'm not taking your girl away with me."

About that time, Elvis made her do automatic writing. This is a recognized form of mediumship in which an alleged spirit communicates by forcing the hand of a psychic individual to write, usually very rapidly and with his own style and handwriting rather than the living partner's. Dorothy showed me some samples, which were pretty rough scribbles. Still, I could clearly make out a line reading, "Not to be afraid . . . love her . . . need her . . . ask Holzer . . . teach you about the Other Side."

There was no holding Dorothy back now. Her mother

recalled an old friend who had sometimes mentioned me, and the contact was made.

Dorothy came to see me once a week, and in between she was to keep notes of her encounters with Elvis. If anything unusual happened, she was to telephone me long distance. Her astral flights with Elvis continued and she took careful notes of their conversations.

There was one thing in particular that Elvis kept impressing on her. He didn't like people impersonating him and using his name as a "ladder." But Dorothy assured him there was nothing she could do about it. Who would listen to *her*?

Elvis then took her on an astral flight to Graceland.

"We were out behind the house and I walked right into the wrought-iron furniture and I bruised my knee," Dorothy said and showed me the physical bruise she had as a result. "It was a low table with a glass top, and I smacked right into it, and it sure hurt. This happened June 1."

I later established that the wrought-iron table does in fact exist, exactly where Dorothy had smacked into it in the astral plane. Also, it would have been nearly impossible for to her have known this, as his garden furniture is not widely publicized.

Their journey always started out the same way: up from the couch (and out of her physical body) and then through the tunnel. Next, she found herself crossing a bridge, after which she glided into a room with large, white columns. Crossing another, smaller bridge, they then found themselves in a beautiful park. There were other people there, too, but Dorothy did not know them. Some were in clothes of an earlier period, others in robes. There was a diffused kind of light around them. Then, all of a sudden, she went through another tunnel with Elvis, and she found herself in the driveway of his home. That's when they went around to the back of the house where Dorothy bumped into the garden furniture.

All this material is similar to what Dr. Raymond Moody discovered when researching his bestselling book *Life After Life,* a collection of stories about people who were temporally or clinically considered dead, but who managed to revive themselves to life despite the odds against their survival. Accounts of going through tunnels with bright lights have also been retold to me by many people with bona fide experiences involving visits to what we usually call "the world beyond." One can argue that Dorothy Sherry *may* have read these books—but did she? I think not. She came to me to be reassured that her visitations from Elvis were not hallucinatory, not to gain notoriety or profit.

Bumping into the wrought-iron table in Elvis's backyard brought Dorothy back into her body instantly, leaving her with a terrific headache and a bruised leg.

How do they get back into Dorothy's world?

"We come back through a tunnel. It takes longer coming back than going and he helps me down, then I open my eyes and I can still see him and he'll wave and say, 'I'll see you tomorrow night.' He then just walks away . . . into nothing. I always feel exhausted afterwards."

I asked Dorothy what else Elvis had told her about himself.

"They called him 'the King' and he felt he was in his own home so he sometimes was rough on people. He would scream and rant and always have his own way. Now he is sorry he acted that way. He took a lot of drugs, but he didn't kill himself, he says. He only got himself on a track where instead of taking two pills, he would take six. Subconsciously, he wanted to die. He was very unhappy, very lonely. But he says it may have been through his own fault, his moods."

By now I pressed for some detail about his private life that could not be known to Dorothy, or for that matter to me or to anyone in the outside world. Dorothy hemmed and hawed and finally said, yes, there was something he did as a little boy. He *peed* on the wall!

Later, I discovered that he had been reprimanded for smearing *peanut* butter on the wall. Could she have misunderstood the word?

On June 9, Elvis came to Dorothy in my study. After some preliminaries, I asked if he had a message for anyone.

"He says, he sends his apologies to Sonny West, Red's cousin . . . if they felt hurt in any way, he didn't mean it."

The names meant nothing to me, but I have since realized they are two of the authors of a recent book about Elvis.

I asked what Elvis was doing on the Other Side, when he wasn't taking Dorothy on astral visits. "Working on some of his songs, still trying to improve them," Dorothy replied. "They do give concerts over there, but of course, they don't have records. When I asked who was in charge, Elvis replied they called them 'the teachers' and that above them was 'the All-Knowing.' "

"Elvis says he has always known there was a God, and there is. He doesn't know though if God is a person. He still feels ignorant and he is going to school over there."

I asked if Elvis's mother was with him all the time, but it appears she is on a higher level of consciousness while Elvis is still on the first.

I then wondered if Elvis had gotten through to anyone else except Dorothy since this passing. After all, I've received messages from the King. Not one of them proved worthy of belief.

"He's gotten through to his father, in the dream state, and told him to stop the counterfeit Elvis Presleys, and to keep an eye on his daughter. This was in January of this year. Only one psychic has had contact with him, someone named Wright. But he says, I wouldn't pay attention to her, sir. He means you."

I thought this was as good a time as any to ask for the essence of Elvis's message to the world.

"Please make people aware of the Other Side, that we are not dead. Life goes on. This is only a bus stop. There are so many over here who want to communicate, but people don't understand . . . *death is not the end!"*

I then examined some of Dorothy's notes, taken at her own home immediately on awakening from one of her astral excursions with Elvis.

On June 11, she remarked that he talked about his ability with karate and showed her some of his kicks. (I discovered much later that David, his bodyguard, had also taught him karate.)

"Elvis is concerned about his father's health, taking care of his affairs may be too much for him. And tell the Colonel, he is glad he is making money, but isn't enough, enough?"

In an earlier entry, May 26, Dorothy visited Elvis's home again.

"I saw a red sectional couch and a very massive kitchen. Outside, somewhere on the grounds, was a big fountain with colored lights."

The next day she discovered that Elvis had his cologne "specially mixed" and, on May 29, Elvis even decided to watch Ella Fitzgerald on the Johnny Carson show with

Dorothy! He liked her gospel songs, and as I was later to learn, he sang gospel songs himself.

"I found it amusing," Dorothy wrote, "that he stood and watched television. As we turned to leave, the room got suddenly bright, like the sun coming from behind a cloud; as we crossed over, it got brighter and brighter. I asked Elvis what it was and he only said that it was 'His essence.' We walked for a while and saw other couples who Elvis told me were couples like ourselves who had made contact."

On June 14, Elvis came through as soon as Dorothy had sat down on the couch in my study. According to her, he was wearing a black cashmere sweater this time. When I asked him to tell me exactly what he wanted done about his affairs, Dorothy was quick to reply.

"He's concerned about his father. Heart trouble, and there is also something wrong with his circulatory system. He says there's been enough sideshow activities and souvenirs. I'm a private man. I want them off my property. There's plenty outside for them to buy. I don't want them walking around my mama's grave. This is like a sideshow, a zoo. They have to realize I was a person and not some kind of god."

Dorothy was now less concerned about her sanity, as I had long since convinced her that hers was an apparently genuine case of spirit communication. But now she worried lest the world would not believe her, and by implication, she would be letting Elvis down. I understood her concern, knowing full well that the will to disbelieve is very strong when people are afraid to alter their basic philosophies, and I encouraged her to request additional bits and pieces of personal information that would help us make the identification of Elvis Presley even stronger than it already was.

During the last week of June, Dorothy came up with some additional information jotted down the morning after an astral flight with Elvis.

"Fay Harris was a friend of his mother's in Tupelo . . . and his aunt's name is Tressie and she's living . . . and his uncle Vestor married his aunt Clitis, they were his father's brother and his mother's sister. Oh, and his car caught fire once when he just started on his way to a show in a small town. And he's met Bill Black, a bass player who had started out with him . . . and his mother once tore up a pair of very dirty sneakers when he was in his early teens."

The material was certainly private and not the sort of thing one finds in books about a celebrity. I asked Dorothy if she could recall a particular place in detail, other than Graceland.

"The Hilton Hotel in Las Vegas," she replied without a moment's hesitation. "He took me backstage to his dressing room. It has in it a couch, a large mirror over a table, and there's an elevator which runs behind it, off the hallway, so he can get on stage without being seen by the crowds. Oh, and something funny, the parking lot is in front of the hotel—not behind, not below, but actually in front."

It wasn't until the seance of July 13 that this data was confirmed as correct by David Stanley, who had been there. But Dorothy had never been to Las Vegas! How could she have known?

When we finally met with the family for that seance, Dorothy was a bundle of nerves. Just like Elvis, she is a very private person. I assured her that nobody was interested in anything but the truth, and she did not have to perform like a trained circus elephant. After all, Dorothy was not a publicity-hungry professional clairvoyant with an eye toward making headlines, but a simple housewife and mother, who just happened to be psychic and somehow fell into this bizarre situation very much against her will.

But since she seemed a little nervous, I gave her a light suggestion, not deep hypnosis but merely a form of relaxation therapy I often use with tense individuals. At the same time, I noticed that her face seemed to take on another person's characteristics. The more relaxed she became, the more the communication proceeded.

Here then is the exact transcript of what transpired in that significant seance confrontation with Elvis Presley on July 13, 1978, nearly a year after he left the physical world.

H.H.: Would you all uncross your legs and relax. If you want to take your shoes off, take your shoes off. Just whatever you want. Be in a quiet, receptive state. You are among friends. We are here to do an experiment —we are opening the door to a man whose contact is desired. We're well aware of the fact that the contact is desired from his side to us and not from us to him. We therefore invite Mr. Presley to make himself known in whatever manner he wishes, to any of us, in any way he sees fit from his standpoint. We offer our services, and willingness to make the contact.

[*Several minutes of silence.*]

H.H.: I therefore call upon Elvis Presley, if he be present, to make himself known in whatever manner he sees fit or suitable to impress Dorothy (and me) whom he has impressed many times before—or any one of us—if that is more to his liking. Our purpose is not to pry, but to make the communication possible in such a way that his intentions are served above all, that his message is carried across to those who care, and, in so doing, that we reemphasize his identity and continuing existence in a dimension beyond the three-dimensional one.

Dorothy, I would like you to be very relaxed and receptive and I would like you to open yourself up to his coming as you have many times before. And though some of the things I may ask you have come before and are therefore known to you from previous visits by him, by Mr. Presley, I would nevertheless sum it up in this manner.

D.S.: He's here now.

H.H.: Has he anything to say?

D.S.: There's a whole pack of them here.

H.H.: Are any of them connected with him?

D.S.: His mother is here.

H.H.: Can you describe his mother?

D.S.: She's short, she's shorter than I am, sad eyes.

H.H.: What color eyes?

D.S.: I don't know.

H.H.: How's she dressed?

D.S.: In a—I don't know what you'd call it—house dress, it's plain, and it's got a belt around the middle. She's very blurry.

H.H.: Does he have anything to say as an opening remark before we go further?

D.S.: He's laughing.

H.H.: Why's he laughing?

D.S.: Giggles. He wants to know if the Colonel has Ok'd this interview.

H.H.: I'm sure he has or we wouldn't be here.

D.S.: He meant that jokingly.

H.H.: Does he wish to elaborate?

D.S.: No, he's just laughing his fool-head off.

H.H.: There are here, apart from you, there are three other people. I hope he's satisfied with their coming.

D.S.: He says he hopes they are satisfied with *his* coming.

H.H.: Well, that would depend to a large degree on him.

D.S.: He's being very . . . silly, no, uh, smart and I don't know why.

H.H.: He is aware, of course, what we're trying to do and why it's important that he's here.

D.S.: Yes.

H.H.: He is aware of the fact that *he* has arranged all of this and no one else has?

D.S.: Yes.

H.H.: Very well, then it's our intention to do the best we can with what we have on hand. We need his help and cooperation.

D.S.: Yes, sir. Anything I can do. He wants to know, I don't know who he's . . . Charley! Where's Charley. Who's Charley?

H.H.: I don't know any Charley.

D.S.: And did his father see a doctor?

H.H.: I don't know the answer, I did pass the message on.

D.S.: I'll have to find out for myself.

H.H.: Is there anything about his father he wishes to tell us?

D.S.: He thinks his father is overworking but that he's becoming almost as well known as himself.

H.H.: In what way?

D.S.: He has written articles.

H.H.: Well, what about the rest of his family?

D.S.: What about them?

H.H.: Any comment he wishes to make?

D.S.: No.

H.H.: Does he approve or disapprove of anything that's going on?

D.S.: I never saw him here, is there a *cousin here* or am I wrong because his mother said something that I can't quite . . .

H.H.: Why has he brought her?

D.S.: He didn't bring her, she's brought him. Trying to make sure he behaved himself. [*Laughter.*]

H.H.: Ask him to talk a little about the conditions under which he now lives.

D.S.: He says, exactly what do you want to know?

H.H.: Ask him, what are your afterlife conditions exactly like, from day to day.

D.S.: They go to a school, everybody has a job to do.

H.H.: What is his job?

D.S.: He's watching over me.

H.H.: What is your link from the past?

D.S.: We were married before.

H.H.: How does he feel about reincarnation?

D.S.: He says you can certainly believe it, and this is the whole point to this meeting. He says if people would just believe it, it would change the world and mankind wouldn't be so damn stupid.

H.H.: Anybody present who would be interested in reincarnation other than you and I?

D.S.: I think it's the lady.

H.H.: Is he pointing at anyone?

D.S.: No, he's pacing up and down.

H.H.: Has he ever discussed reincarnation with anyone while he was in the physical state?

D.S.: Oh yes, many times.

H.H.: With whom?

D.S.: With everybody, with his father and his friends. And he says he believed that with his mind he could do many things. It isn't as strong as he believed it was then. He found out he was only a novice. I'm losing him, I'm sorry. I'm getting too nervous.

H.H.: Relax; there's nothing to be nervous about, but would you ask him to steady you. I ask Mr. Presley to please steady her. This is your instrument, you must help me steady her.

D.S.: "I told you she's a baby."

H.H.: You're doing fine but you must help us steady her. Are you in control again? Is he next to you now?

D.S.: No, he's pacing up and down behind uh—[*points to David Stanley*].

H.H.: I would like you to ask Mr. Presley what his connection is to the gentleman, if any.

D.S.: Cousin.

H.H.: Is there anything he wishes to tell us about the gentleman, anything that has occurred between them that we would be very interested in discussing?

D.S.: My grandmother is here now, she's talking.

H.H.: Tell your grandmother to butt out.

D.S.: You don't tell my grandmother to butt out.

H.H.: And kindly stay out, that we have a specific line of inquiry which must be continued; thank you.

D.S.: No, she's still here.

H.H.: Why, what does she have to contribute to this line of inquiry?

D.S.: She says she's here to help if she can.

H.H.: Fine, she's welcome.

D.S.: She says she doesn't butt out for anybody.

H.H.: All right, I'll take it back, but we must stick with the line.

D.S.: She says he's a good boy, leave him alone.

H.H.: Who's a good boy?

D.S.: Elvis.

H.H.: Where's Elvis right now?

D.S.: He's back now.

H.H.: Would you ask him to please come forward again and answer some questions that will be most important to what he's trying to do.

D.S.: He says he's sorry. [*Laughter*].

H.H.: Is he listening to me now?

D.S.: Yes.

H.H.: As far as the gentleman is concerned who is sitting opposite you now, I would like to know if there was anything between them in the way of friendship.

D.S.: Why am I getting a cousin, and then a half-brother?

H.H.: Well, stay with it and don't please question what you're getting.

D.S.: Did someone use a camera on stage during one of the last concerts, someone wrote a poem later, after. He says, 'Hell, they know I'm here.'

H.H.: Who's they?

D.S.: These people.

H.H.: I'd like to know how he feels about this gentleman.

D.S.: Likes him, almost loves him.

H.H.: Have they done anything together that is important? Ever perform a service for him that was very important at any time?

D.S.: He's standing there laughing. He is standing there laughing his fool head off. He wants it to come across that he wants people to believe that they exist, that they are alive, that they are well, and that they want to communicate with their loved ones. This was the whole purpose, he said.

H.H.: I would like to ask him, while we are on the subject—much as I appreciate him being on the Other Side—there were certain things he liked in this world. Can he talk about some of his favorite possessions?

D.S.: His daughter was his favorite possession.

H.H.: Have you been to his daughter's room with him?

D.S.: No, I've been up in his house.

H.H.: What did you see at the house?

D.S.: I saw his grandmother and some lady who is taking care of his grandmother. She's a very little lady. She's old, she's wrinkled, she's kind of like hunched over.

H.H.: Is she there now?

D.S.: Oh yes.

H.H.: What is in back of the house?

D.S.: It looked like a handball court and it's played with a racquet, and I saw a chain-link fence and there was wrought-iron furniture directly behind in the yard.

H.H.: Were you in Las Vegas with him?

D.S.: Yes.

H.H.: What did the thing look like he took you to?

D.S.: It was a very tall hotel and the parking lot was in the front of the hotel. I kept trying to reject that— here I was, then we went inside, we passed a beautiful lobby, we went off and we made a turn, we were inside a room with a very big stage. I was on that stage. I was also behind it. It's a hallway that has a back elevator where he can go down without having to go through the lobby, without having to go through those people and be mobbed, he was very afraid towards the end of being hurt.

H.H.: Hurt by whom?

D.S.: Fans, crazy people.

H.H.: Was he ever harmed by a fan?

D.S.: In Texas.

H.H.: What happened?

D.S.: He was practically mauled, in the beginning they would tear his clothes all the time. Now that he thinks back it was quite funny.

H.H.: Did he think that someone would harm him physically?

D.S.: Yes, he was afraid. There were threats. Threats against his daughter. He wants to know how his daughter is.

H.H.: Was he ever physically threatened or thought he was in danger of his life?

D.S.: Yes, there were phone calls, there was some kind of communication where his father . . .

H.H.: A particular situation where his life really was in danger and somebody had to help him?

D.S.: Somebody jumped up on stage. Thought he was being threatened. Went into a total panic.

H.H.: Then what happened?

D.S.: His friends, or so-called friends, they're not his friends anymore. Hell, doesn't even want to discuss them. Quickly pushed, knocked him off the stage.

H.H.: Was there anybody in particular who helped him?

D.S.: Doesn't want to talk about them. They wrote a book that he hopes his father is doing something about—or the Colonel. He thought they were his friends, that they were loyal to him. He's been hurt.

H.H.: By whom?

D.S.: Red, Sonny, David.

H.H.: What about them?

D.S.: There's three of them, they turned against me, they twisted everything and blew it up. Why would they want to talk about me like that?

H.H.: This threat to his life.

D.S.: He wants to get them someday.

H.H.: How does he feel about impersonators?

D.S.: Oh lordie, he says, ok. He doesn't want them. He says he worked hard, getting where he was and he started from nothing. Why should they use his name. He wants them to stop. He thought you told him that was being taken care of. He's talking to you.

H.H.: I think it is being taken care of.

D.S.: Then why are they still around?

H.H.: These things take time.

D.S.: He says they stink.

H.H.: I'm inclined to agree with him.

D.S.: He says if I ever looked like that I'd never walk on a stage again.

H.H.: Is he interested in psychic healing?

D.S.: Yes. Yes. "I believed I could heal."

H.H.: Did he have the ability?

D.S.: He says he believed he could heal. He says if he had more time.

H.H.: What about his interest in healing?

D.S.: He was interested in everything.

H.H.: Did he himself have the power of psychic healing?

D.S.: He believed he did.

H.H.: Did he ever discuss it with anybody?

D.S.: Yes, with his friends, with his associates. He believed there was something with a leg, and he healed it.

H.H.: Who broke a leg?

D.S.: Somebody's son, skiing.

H.H.: You mentioned something about his hands being peculiar in some way.

D.S.: Bites his nails, he bit his nails or he bites his nails. He still does. The ends of his fingers are extremely rough and the side of his hand is extremely rough.

H.H.: How is that so?

D.S.: I don't know, karate?

H.H.: Did he do that by himself?

D.S.: No, no he used to work out.

H.H.: With whom?

D.S.: Dave, Sonny, you know those guys we talked about before.

H.H.: What is it that he's complaining about, so we can specify it. I'd like to be sharp about it.

D.S.: "I'm not complaining about anything."

H.H.: But I have the impression he is. Could it be a misunderstanding about certain things?

D.S.: He says there's one thing he couldn't misunderstand.

H.H.: And what is that?

D.S.: It's that book.

H.H.: What is it in that book that he objects to?

D.S.: From the first page to the last.

H.H.: What elements are there, something in it that isn't true?

D.S.: "From the first page to the last. They were my friends, they hurt me, by writing that book."

H.H.: Why?

D.S.: "They made me sound like I should be in a home, that I was crazy. I was a little crazy, we're all a little crazy. You all know that."

H.H.: Is it that he doesn't like to have books written about him?

D.S.: "This book, they were my friends, don't you understand?"

H.H.: They'd have to be your friends to write about you—they had to know you, a stranger couldn't do it.

D.S.: "They wrote lies, they blew it up, turned on me. They hurt me, they hurt me. I trusted them. I trusted them with my life."

H.H.: Which ones?

D.S.: "Do I have to say it again: Red, Sonny, Dave."

H.H.: Your objection is to some of the things in the book?

D.S.: "Everything in the book."

H.H.: Would you like that someone else would write a book that would rectify matters?

D.S.: "My family. Tell the Colonel he should finally write that book."

H.H.: What about anyone else, what about your family—books are being written already.

D.S.: "Hundreds of them, but they're not me."

H.H.: Did you like jewelry?

D.S.: "Yes."

H.H.: Anything in particular?

D.S.: "There's a diamond cross."

H.H.: What kind of diamond cross?

D.S.: "All diamonds."

H.H.: What's it look like?

D.S.: "Like a cross."

H.H.: One diamond?

D.S.: "Not one diamond, all diamonds" . . . he's talking about something else now, something about Ginger. She was supposed to give it to Lisa.

H.H.: What kind of jewelry?

D.S.: A bracelet.

H.H.: What kind?

D.S.: She was supposed to give it to Lisa, and she hasn't given it to Lisa.

H.H.: Is this a message?

D.S.: Yes, tell her to give it to Lisa. It's a promise. She's keeping it. She's doing all right for herself. She's always in the paper, in the movies. She's doing all right. How's Linda?

H.H.: What is the bracelet like?

D.S.: He wants to know how Linda is, he doesn't want to talk about the bracelet now.

H.H.: Linda, I understand she's well, but can't you go there yourself?

D.S.: He can't be bothered now, he's busy.

H.H.: Any other jewelry of his own he wants to talk about now?

D.S.: He's turning from one mood to the other, he does that often.

H.H.: I would like him to make a statement because I want to tell the world what his desire is at this time.

D.S.: He wants people to learn to acknowledge that he (or we) exist because there are many lonely people

who want to talk to loved ones and because of total
ignorance, utter and complete ignorance—they're
fools, they don't learn.

H.H.: I agree with him, this is my message too.

D.S.: "They don't learn. Maybe, someday, with your
help I can help these people. This is all I want to talk
about. This is all I want to discuss. Give my daddy a
kiss." (*Then, looking directly at David*) "A hug and a
kiss. Tell him he's all right, and he's happy, and he'll
be around."

H.H.: Would you ask him to please talk further to the
two people, the lady and the gentleman, and say
whatever he wishes. They've come a long way to be
here with him.

D.S.: He appreciates that.

H.H.: It would be courteous to talk to them awhile, he
may say whatever he wishes.

D.S.: He wants them to give him a hug or a kiss. Tell
him he loves him, after all, he's my daddy he hasn't
been well, he wants them to look after him because
he can't interfere, he's tired, and because of this ignorance just can't. He says he wants an answer—watch
after his father.

H.H.: You want the gentleman to speak, yes, he will
take the message.

D.S.: This lady he talked to on the phone. He's fading
again, I'm losing him!

H.H.: I will bring him back.

D.S.: His mouth is moving, I can see him, but I can't
hear him. I'm sorry.

H.H.: Mr. Presley, please pull your emotions together.
It is very important that you stay.

D.S.: He's pacing, I don't know what's the matter with him. He's impatient.

H.H.: There are things that you can tell us, that you're debating with yourself.

D.S.: He has touched this lady, his hand is on her shoulder.

H.H.: Now?

D.S.: Right now.

H.H.: Has he touched her before?

D.S.: No, not since we've gotten here, if that's what you mean.

H.H.: No, at another time.

D.S.: He has touched them all before, he has been there and no one noticed. "They don't understand that we're here."

H.H.: But they can't see him.

D.S.: They can if they wish.

H.H.: How?

D.S.: "Open up, and they will see me, for I will be there."

H.H.: Is there anything specific that he wants them to do?

D.S.: Just his daddy.

H.H.: What about the lady, she's come a long way to be here, he must have some remarks to address to her, perhaps to the rest of her family.

D.S.: He had a phone call.

H.H.: Who made the call, explain.

D.S.: He called her.

H.H.: While he was in the flesh?

D.S.: He's shaking his head at me, I'm not getting all of it.

H.H.: Is the phone call important?

D.S.: Yes.

H.H.: What did it deal with?

D.S.: I'm starting to burn again, I'm sorry.

H.H.: He is close to you. Mr. Presley, please, what was the phone call about, why did you mention it?

D.S.: Hans, I can't hear him.

H.H.: Is he still with you?

D.S.: Yes.

H.H.: He's probably getting excited, if you feel very hot. I would ask that the guides, who are arranging this meeting, stand by, calm the atmosphere, to make communication possible.

D.S.: God, I'm burning.

H.H.: Mr. Presley, will you please calm down. You used to take directions, please take directions from me. Now calm down, stand still, and we will continue to speak calmly.

D.S.: He wants to know how come I feel him and no one else can. Does it have to do with our past link?

H.H.: It has to do with physical ability as well—in the solar plexus area of head and stomach—you know already, you've been taught this in school, but you must be calm or you will be unable to communicate. Now please, Mr. Presley, go behind the lady and leave the instrument for a minute. Do as I tell you.

D.S.: I'm burning, Hans, I'm burning.

H.H.: Please let go of the instrument for a second so that we can resume communication.

D.S.: He says he doesn't understand.

H.H.: What?

D.S.: Why is he so hot this time?

H.H.: Because there has been worry and resistance and the energies being drawn, and you're upset.

D.S.: He's not moving and I'm burning.

H.H.: There is nothing to worry about. Give me your hands, please. Calm, relax completely.

D.S.: He's not moving, he says he's here to protect me.

H.H.: I know.

D.S.: And that he's not going to move.

H.H.: Calm yourself, Mr. Presley, please stay where you are for one second. Disconnect, please. Then reconnect. Disconnect, then reconnect.

D.S.: What's happening, I don't know what's happening.

H.H.: He's trying to get you into trance, let go, it's all right.
He has something more to say. Please let go of the instrument and go over to the lady for a second.

D.S.: I've never felt anything like this before. He's very intense.

H.H.: Because there are people present who mean something to him and he cannot control his emotions. Now break the circuit. Mr. Presley, please go behind the lady opposite me and touch her.

D.S.: I can't see him.

H.H.: I want you to stand in back of the lady now and touch her and to calm yourself because we are not going to get any place unless you do. I know it's difficult—you will have to learn to take directions here.

D.S.: I'm getting a name, something about a psychic named Wright—I can't see him anymore, Hans. He's going in and out.

H.H.: Does he have anything further to tell us? Just calm yourself down for a couple of minutes. Let go completely, relax.

D.S.: I'm starting to burn again.

H.H.: Mr. Presley, will you please stand behind the lady again and you are to relax, let go, and not worry about it anymore.

D.S.: I'm getting hot again, hot.

H.H.: He's emotionally upset, he's trying to push something through.

D.S.: But what?

H.H.: Well, that's what we're here for, to try and find out.

D.S.: I can't see him anymore and I'm burning.

H.H.: Is there something about a cologne or perfume, do you remember it?

D.S.: I remember it but I can't hear him anymore.

H.H.: What is it about the perfume?

D.S.: He had it specially blended.

H.H.: By whom, what was it like?

D.S.: Sweet.

H.H.: The particular scent.

D.S.: I never smelled anything like it before, it's always in my house.

H.H.: Describe it.

D.S.: It's different.

H.H.: What other parts of the house have you been in?

D.S.: The front hall, black and white tiles in the front hall.

H.H.: Did you see him wear any jewelry at any time?

D.S.: No, and he has no suits, just regular trousers or a white shirt.

H.H.: Did he ever tell anybody he trusted them with his life?

D.S.: Yes.

H.H.: Who?

D.S.: I can't hear him but he's here.

H.H.: Let me address him directly. Mr. Presley, do you have anything further to tell us?

D.S.: He says he loves these people, he's not angry, he's sorry. Because he's very hot-tempered. He's coming back, because I can see him.

H.H.: He's calming down, I'm sure.

D.S.: This is much stronger than before.

H.H.: Not to worry—Mr. Presley, you understand the need for calm at this particular moment.

D.S.: He says he's trying to help me, he doesn't want to hurt, he doesn't understand what happened. Would you please explain.

H.H.: Well it is his pent-up emotions and some frustration which somehow got out of hand and got into Dorothy because you are holding onto her.

D.S.: "I'll always hold onto her, I don't understand."

H.H.: It's a mechanical thing, you are not at fault.

D.S.: "You think I will eventually learn. I'm being taught some things."

H.H.: Yes.

D.S.: Eventually, he says, I'm just a stupid southern boy.

H.H.: You're learning very well, you know already a great deal—not to worry about it.

D.S.: He says I'm learning more each day, I'm trying, he doesn't understand what happened to Dot. He doesn't want to hurt me. Is he hurting me?

H.H.: Not any longer—it's a mechanical thing that happened.

D.S.: He doesn't want to hurt anybody, he never wanted to hurt anybody. And he's starting up again and I'm burning again.

H.H.: No anger please! It would help if he talked about something very unemotional now, would he please talk about psychic healing, how he feels about it.

D.S.: He's pacing again, he's back and forth in front of this couch.

H.H.: Mr. Presley, you have to calm yourself to communicate, there's no other way, and the way to do this is by changing the subject matter.

D.S.: He says I'll walk away if that will help.

H.H.: No, stay, but change the subject.

D.S.: He likes to touch me.

H.H.: Then touch her.

D.S.: He's afraid, he's afraid he's going to hurt me.

H.H.: He can touch you.

D.S.: He always hangs onto me, he says he's my security blanket and that's true. I hang onto him. He says she's a child she has to hold onto me—am I going to hurt her if I grab her?

H.H.: The answer is no.

D.S.: "All right sir, she trusts you, I trust you."

H.H.: Is there something we ought to know that you haven't told us?

D.S.: He only wants people to know, to acknowledge that he is here, he is here, he is whole, he is well—he is here with momma. She is well, she's not quite as happy, but he doesn't know why. She blames herself for his early death—she blames herself. She failed him.

H.H.: How has she failed him?

D.S.: She doesn't think she was a very good mother.

H.H.: Why not?

D.S.: Overpowered, she drank, she drank. She's very

sorry. She's getting upset now. What is going on? Is it people from home that are causing this?

H.H.: They have only love for him.

D.S.: Maybe it's bringing it back.

H.H.: Any unresolved issue between him and the people from home, anything unfinished?

D.S.: He didn't finish his life.

H.H.: I mean in the relationship.

D.S.: There are ties, of all kinds, bringing us back.

H.H.: What kind of ties?

D.S.: He doesn't want to bring it back, he has a lot of hurt.

H.H.: Who hurt him?

D.S.: People hurt him.

H.H.: Who specifically?

D.S.: His momma was hurt.

H.H.: By whom?

D.S.: His momma was hurt by family, something to do with family. They didn't care, she had nothing to eat, I'm sorry. He's going out again—at my shoulder.

H.H.: Don't move.

D.S.: He's leaving, he's leaving. I'm losing him—he's still here, touching me.

H.H.: I don't want him to leave in anger or upset. We will give him some energy.

D.S.: Someone better give me some energy because I'm losing him, he's got my shoulder.

H.H.: Give me your hands, take the energy you need.

D.S.: He's got very big hands.

H.H.: Why is he upset?

D.S.: He doesn't feel this is going the way it should.

H.H.: How does he want it to go?

D.S.: "There's been enough written about me. The

whole world knows about me. I have no privacy, at least let me have some. Please, please."

H.H.: The reason for the conversation is not invasion of privacy but proof of identity to an unbelieving, foolish world—nothing to harm you.

D.S.: He doesn't care what they think about him, it is unimportant.

H.H.: It's not unimportant.

D.S.: He wants to know if they can remember singing the gospel songs . . . all night long, do you remember?

H.H.: Where?

D.S.: Home, hotels, anywhere, he loved to sing the gospel songs. His momma loved the gospel songs.

H.H.: What about these people present here?

D.S.: He says he loves them. He loves them all. He wants his business taken care of. He wants the people off his property, he wants the garbage thrown about his momma's grave stopped.

H.H.: What garbage?

D.S.: How they do that. He says they're like wolves. He doesn't want this. Get them off his property. That's the only place he had any privacy.

H.H.: What else does he want?

D.S.: He wants his daughter looked after.

H.H.: By whom?

D.S.: Pris, her mother. He wants his father to have some say with Lisa. The only thing he regrets is he wanted his daughter to have a home life. He's afraid she's going to grow up wrong. He's crying. My God, he's crying.

H.H.: We'll do whatever we can to carry out his wishes.

D.S.: His little girl, I'm sorry [*starts to sob*]. He says

he's sorry he's putting me through this and he says it always seems he's saying I'm sorry.

H.H.: What's he sorry about?

D.S.: He can't do anything right, he's sorry he's not cooperating. He's sorry for what he's doing to me.

H.H.: He is cooperating.

D.S.: He says he does not want to upset me needlessly. I'm all he's got, but I'm *not* all he's got. He's always been alone . . . and his daughter is always going to be alone—[*crying*].

H.H.: Is there something he wants the two people here to do about all this?

D.S.: Look after his little girl, his baby, his wife—don't let Pris hurt her, he doesn't want her in a boarding school. He wants her to have love. He's all upset. His momma's back.

H.H.: Has she anything to say?

D.S.: She's holding him.

H.H.: Mr. Presley, I will have to release the instrument unless you have something further to say.

D.S.: [*Crying*]

H.H.: [*To the guests*] Anything you want to ask him? Then it is best if he withdrew.

D.S.: "No, I'm not leaving Dot."

H.H.: It's best if you separate now.

D.S.: You don't understand, he says.

H.H.: What don't I understand?

D.S.: "We need each other."

H.H.: But we cannot accomplish any more because you are too upset emotionally. It would be best to try another time.

D.S.: No.

H.H.: What does he want to do?

D.S.: He wants people to learn, Hans, that's why he wanted me to see you.

H.H.: Of course they will learn.

D.S.: They are not going to believe.

H.H.: Those who are ready to believe, will, and those who are not, will not. It's their karma, we cannot force them in anyway.

D.S.: [*Sobbing*]

H.H.: In the name of all who loved you, we ask you to let go, and to separate from your instrument.

D.S.: He doesn't understand why I'm so upset.

H.H.: You're just reflecting his own feelings, there's nothing to worry about.

D.S.: [*Shrieks, pain*]

H.H.: I ask that the guides come forward and protect the instrument so that the instrument may be released.

D.S.: He says, but I love her.

H.H.: That's understood.

D.S.: "I don't want to leave."

H.H.: You must, for the moment only.

D.S.: "I was left alone. My God, my momma left me alone—I was left alone with nobody. I won't leave her alone."

H.H.: You will be with her again.

D.S.: "You're not sending me away permanently?"

H.H.: No.

D.S.: "For sure?"

H.H.: My word—just for now, so that we can refresh ourselves. Go in peace, go in peace, with our love and understanding, with the right to return at all times—go with our blessings, and our prayers.

When the seance ended, Dorothy, still in a state of great agitation that she herself could not understand, asked for a glass of water. She felt hot and shaky, a state she had never been in before. As soon as her equilibrium was restored, I escorted her to the elevator and then returned to the suite.

David Stanley, who had initially been negative toward the entire encounter, was now a changed man. He readily confirmed many of the things that had been said through Dorothy's mediumship, and added that he himself had actually realized that Elvis was pacing up and down behind him, just Dorothy had claimed. As for Dee Presley, her strict religious outlook made it difficult for her to accept spirit communication outside the religious establishment, and she was frank in admitting she did not "believe in" reincarnation, a cardinal point in Elvis's message and continued existence on the Other Side.

Despite this, she was visibly impressed with what had just transpired in her presence.

"That phone call," she kept saying to us, "if she could only get more about that telephone call—when it was made, and under what circumstances."

I promised Dee I would ask Dorothy to convey this request to Elvis if he should come to her that night.

The following morning, July 15, Dorothy called me in great agitation. "I've got your answer," she said, explaining that Elvis was pleased with our seance, but at the same time frank in admitting he had been extremely agitated by the presence of two family members: the stepbrother, close friend, and body-guard with whom he had shared so much of his life, and the stepmother who knew so much of his personal dilemma. But, Dorothy told me on the telephone, there had been a lot of anger and fighting between Elvis and Dee—he had resented the marriage of his father's at first, feeling it had come too soon after his mother died.

But what about the telephone call, I pressed. Under what circumstances was it made?

"It's connected with a doctor . . . an ambulance . . . the house," Dorothy replied.

The truth of the matter is this: there were two telephone calls that last day of Elvis's life on earth. The first one allegedly was a consuming, heated argument between himself and his stepmother. The second one, moments before his passing, had tried to smooth things over again between them. Only Dee knew this, and, of course, Elvis.

David confessed he had actually heard Elvis's haunting laughter in the room.

"His laughter—that really made me feel like it was happening," said David. "His humor was great. He was always laughing with me. Maybe he was laughing at me because I was sitting here doubting the whole thing at the beginning. He was laughing because he'd expect that of me."

Elvis's relatives came away from the spine-tingling seance absolutely certain that he had been in the room with them. Dee and David both said that at one point, as Elvis's spirit grew agitated, they could actually feel him pacing the room and feel him enter their minds.

"I talked to Elvis—it was unbelievable," said David, Elvis's body-guard for six years.

"As a demonstration of psychic ability, the seance was authentic. It impressed me. The medium used the exact words Elvis had said to me two days before he died:

" 'I'll be around . . . I'll take care of you.' As he was at the seance, that's the way I remember him."

Dee confirmed that she and Vernon Presley had both

received phoned threats against Lisa when she was small. "It has never been published," she said.

The stepmother said she also knew Elvis had tried to contact her just hours before he died. "I did receive information—which only one other person knew—that Elvis tried to reach me on the day of his death."

Added Dee with emotion: "Yes, Elvis was here, I know. The medium touched on things she couldn't have known about my life. It was definitely a psychic contact.

"The subjects he talked about through the medium were the things closest to Elvis's heart. It sent shivers down my spine. I am absolutely convinced I was in the presence of Elvis's spirit."

When David Stanley left the seance, he shook my hand and said, "Elvis would have liked you. He was interested in many of the things you do."

I wish I had known. But it's never too late. Because spirit communication isn't wishful thinking, deliberate fraud, or a hoax: though it can be at times. But when it is real, as it is between Elvis Presley and Dorothy Sherry, it should be told to the world. Every little bit of truth helps.

If there had been any doubt in my mind about the validity of Dorothy Sherry's contact with the late King of Rock, the confrontation with Mr. Presley's family dispelled all doubts. Even Dan Schwartz, a somewhat hard-boiled reporter despite his kind exterior and friendly manner, had to admit that we had indeed some pretty convincing evidence of afterlife communication involving Elvis Presley. Of course, I have been through this kind of evidence and this kind of test many times before, although with people of less public importance than Elvis Presley. However, it is always more difficult to prove the afterlife existence of a celebrity than it is of Uncle Frank, because so much is known about famous people that is accessible to would-be forgers, or even to those who are innocent of any bad intentions but who happen to be picking up information about the celebrity without even being aware of it.

In the case of Dorothy Sherry, however, I had taken every precaution to make sure she had had no access to the material that had come through her, either prior to the seance confrontation, or prior to her meeting me, and I am satisfied that there had been no collusion, no self-deception, nothing but a straight and highly *unwanted* communication between Elvis and herself. It was only gradually that she accepted him, only gradually that she began to trust herself and to lose her fear of being declared mentally incompetent. Perhaps it is to some degree due to my influence that she had finally accepted her own mediumship in the light of what had transpired. Whatever the reasons for her acceptance of that facet of her personality that seemed to be different from the average person, although by no means supernatural, Dorothy's performance at the Hotel Drake was truly outstanding. Not that the material that had come through her earlier, either in my presence at my study or alone at her home, was any less important, but due to the fact that two initially hostile witnesses became convinced of the authenticity of the communication only because of what came through the mouth of Dorothy at that particular seance.

I have commented on the main parallels between what Dorothy said, or rather what Elvis said through Dorothy, and the facts bearing out this information, but there were also a few things that seemed at first unimportant that, in retrospect, should be pointed out as additional and important proof for the authenticity of this communication. Early in the seance, Elvis seemed concerned about the well-being of someone named Charley. It turned out, on inquiry, that Charley had been one of his musicians who had been close to him. Upon the news of Elvis's death, Charley had himself taken ill and had a breakdown, induced by the shock of Elvis's sudden passing. Thus the concern about Charley's well-being can easily be understood. Elvis's casual mentioning of his healing powers, and helping someone who had injured his leg in a skiing accident, proved to be authentic too. Someone connected with Elvis's entourage had fallen and actually broken a leg. Elvis, without realizing why, had applied psychic healing to the injured bone and the bone had healed by itself. David Stanley is the witness who confirmed this fact, something that had not been published anywhere.

I had been somewhat puzzled by Dorothy's reference to the camera that had somehow been important to David Stanley, the man to whom the spirit of Elvis pointed in the early part of the seance. Afterward I learned that David Stanley was not only fond of cameras, he had long held the desire to become a professional photographer. The very same words, "I'll take care of you"—which Elvis had spoken several weeks earlier, prior to his death, to David Stanley—emerged again during the seance when the question of the future came up. Perhaps with a sense of foreboding, Elvis assured his half-brother and bodyguard that, no matter what the future would hold for Elvis, he would always be taken care of.

Before Dorothy ever set foot on Las Vegas soil, she had accurately described the peculiar position of the parking lot at the Hilton Hotel, something that could not be guessed at because it seemed irrational and unusual: the parking lot is indeed in front of the hotel and not behind or below it, as one would expect in so crowded a city as

Las Vegas. That an elevator runs behind Elvis's dressing room at the hotel is something that would hardly interest anyone except those connected with the show business end of the hotel, a fact that is not likely to be found in books or magazines; nevertheless, Dorothy was very specific in describing this particular feature of Elvis's Las Vegas dressing room. She also described the large mirror and the table in the room, and her description of the position of the corridor turned out to be entirely correct.

It was only long after our investigation was closed that Dorothy finally set foot in Las Vegas, more out of curiosity than anything else, to see for herself how much of her visions had in fact been true, still always somewhat the doubter.

Although racquetball is a sport indulged in by a considerable number of people, I myself had never heard of the game nor was I aware of the fact that Mr. Presley had a private racquetball court. Nevertheless, Dorothy was right in describing it as being located in back of Graceland, and her description of the nature and position of the iron garden furniture (over which she stumbled and hurt her knee) also corresponded to the facts, according to the family. The only specific statements made by Dorothy that Dee Presley was unable to account for, concerned a "ten-foot-tall chain fence" and "black and white squares in the entrance hall to the house." However, Dorothy plainly said she also visited a huge ranch house, different from Graceland. It is possible that she was talking about the second house in this instance. How the medium could describe Elvis's grandmother, still very much alive and living in Graceland, as "very small, thin, slightly hunched over, very wrinkled, with a large nose and slightly senile" without ever having seen her or a picture of her, is also a piece of evidence that cannot be easily dismissed. Further, she described that there was water on this property in Tennessee, but neither a pool nor a lake, possibly a brook or a stream, and she saw some large black dogs that looked to her like doberman pinschers guarding the property. And she did all this without ever having physically been in Memphis, Tennessee.

On August 3, 1978, I went to Los Angeles for a week, then returned to New York for a few days before embarking once more for Europe, on August 14, to give a series of seminars on parapsychology in Bavaria and Switzerland. I had no time to check on Dorothy during that period, but I had instructed her to keep an exact record of anything and everything that transpired in my absence, and to forward it to me immediately upon my return from Europe.

Here then is the record of what happened after the seance in which contact with the family had been established, as recorded by Dorothy at her home.

August 8

I've been told three times how to watch my health, by him and his mother. I've also been told that things will be revealed that have never been before that I'm going to need all my strength. He also told me that Dr. Holzer will have his name many times before the public and this, in turn, would lead to the success of all his other projects. He's very concerned and so is his mother because I'm finding it very hard to hold my concentration.

August 9

I have been shown more of the connection between Dr. Holzer and myself from a past life. In Egypt I was a small boy and he was a teacher, a wise man. I would sit at his feet and he would teach me. I know we were slaves and had something to do with the building of tombs or pyramids. Dr. Holzer was excused from this because of age. I know we were often very hungry. I was not excused and had to work very hard and was often beaten by the overseers. I died in my early teens by being crushed to death by large rocks.

August 11

I was told tonight by him that I must learn to overcome my possessiveness and stubbornness, that I am taking steps backwards in this cycle. Elvis told me he took too many steps backwards in this life and has a lot to make up. He said I will be helping him and in turn he will be helping me. Our bond is strong and this is how it must be. He has many things to make up and in a way was happy to give up the physical form. He hopes together we will take many steps forward now, in the spirit world, and our next life, which he said is now sure to be better since we will be together. He said to tell Dr. Holzer many of the people he is concerned with now he has been many times before and that he was always interested in the afterlife and reincarnation, but that he is not using his powers to the fullest. Material things are not that important, something he said he was too concerned with, and I must stop thinking of self.

August 12
He was a soldier named James Armstrong in the Civil War, was killed in action from Kentucky. I was his sweetheart.

August 17
Elvis was just here and I got a terrible feeling something is going to happen to his grandmother. I hope to God I'm wrong.

August 27
We walked a far way through a tunnel that opened to a beautiful lagoon, birds were singing and dogs were playing. There seemed to be about a hundred children around this lagoon, some were dancing, others playing musical instruments, and some were just playing games or reading. A few of them greeted us and hugged Elvis. I asked him if he came here often and he said he did. After a while a gong sounded, and they all ran off through the trees. We passed through the tunnel again and ended up on the dirt road with the white fence on each side. We never walked to the top of the road before, but tonight we did. When we arrived at the top it was much much brighter. There were men and women working at desks, they were all in a row on either side, they seemed to glow with a brightness. Matthew came walking down the road, he was glowing too. He told Elvis I wasn't ready to see this yet. Elvis said to him that he told him to show me everything but Matthew said not yet so we turned and left. We walked back down the road. I met my grandfather, James, there. He told Elvis, he was very proud of me and that he was glad we finally got together. He said that he had to leave that he was going to see my mother. Elvis and I talked about his

mother, he said he only saw her once since he's there. We walked for a while and then I returned.

August 29
A friend, Linda, thirty-two, housewife, who knows nothing of my experiences (as you know I haven't told anyone), came to see me with something she felt she had to ask me. Her question was if I have anything at all to do with Elvis Presley. I asked her why. She told me that all day Tuesday she felt me hanging on her arm and that I was very upset and depressed. So far this is true as I have been upset about the paper. I must tell you she was vacationing at the shore at the time and I was at home. She said she told her mother about the feeling. That evening, she went to bed but couldn't fall asleep; suddenly she found herself on the beach in her nightgown talking to me. She described the nightgown I was wearing that night perfectly. She said I was telling her about some article I was very nervous over and how was I going to tell my husband. After a while Elvis appeared beside me. He asked her to try and calm me down as I was getting gray hair over something stupid. She described the exact Elvis I had been seeing right down to the clothes. I didn't comment on this at all because my mother advised me not to. Tuesday night I crossed over with him but I thought I fell asleep during the meeting."

Now this is a most extraordinary entry. I know for a fact that Dorothy would certainly not discuss with anyone her experiences with Elvis, let alone her coming to see me in New York. To begin with, her husband would not have approved, and even if he had, her neighbors and friends

might have ridiculed her since she lived in a small community where such things as extrasensory perception and
mediumship are not exactly everyday occurrences. Thus I
am satisfied that the friend, Linda, who came to her with
her own dream experience did so not because of anything
that Dorothy had said or done, but because of a bona
fide dream of her own. Clearly, she was picking up on
Dorothy's own thoughts, something not unknown in
parapsychology, and somehow managed to share Dorothy's extrasensory experience with Elvis.

When I first questioned Dorothy I asked her about previous psychic experiences and she pooh-poohed the idea
that she had any ESP. But as I investigated this matter
more closely it became clear to me that Elvis would not
have been able to make an appearance, had he not found
at least a reasonable amount of receptiveness in Dorothy;
the experience involving a relative that I have reported on
earlier in this book also points to at least partial mediumship on the part of Dorothy. But it appears now, judging
from the next entry, that Dorothy had somehow been
picked up by the forces on the other side of the veil to be a
vehicle for the communication that was to come between
Elvis Presley and herself, in some way proving the genuineness of it by representing a totally disinterested party,
someone who was as far from being a professional medium
as anyone could be, and someone who was more likely to
be believed than, let us say, someone interested in national
publicity, as are many mediums, unfortunately.

Here is the entry, which sheds revealing light on Dorothy's selection as the go-between.

August 19, 1978
At this time I want to tell you of a dream that has

been happening to me for about two months after these meetings first started. It is kind of a dream within a dream. His mother is coming to see me night after night for three months, saying she wants me to see her son, to make him know that she is trying to reach him, that if he doesn't stop his way of living and get rid of that girl, he's going to die, and that I have to tell him. I tell her there's no way I could get near him to tell him that, she said I will show you the way; I then turn and ask her why we are going over and over this as it is already too late. She then said if she had only known of our connection before, she might have saved him. I tried to tell her to stop blaming herself but she usually disappears and that ends the dream. I'm only mentioning this now because now she has brought the dream one step further. She shows me how I could have reached him and that once we met face to face we would know each other. I would mention her name and that she wants to talk to him by going up to the stage and saying this. He would have one of his men take my name and phone. A week later he would call me and I would meet him at the cargo section at Newark Airport on his plane. The interior of the plane is red, that is all I remember, except for him. Everything happens just as she said it would. I asked her again why she is showing me all this as it is too late and she just disappears.

I too wondered why Presley's mother took the trouble of showing Dorothy the steps she could have taken to prevent Elvis's death except for one thing: if Mrs. Presley has continued feelings of guilt, or perhaps only the sin of omission, exteriorizing this in the dream form might very well discharge her karmic liability. At the same time, it would help cement a closer relationship between herself and Dorothy on the one hand, and herself and her son on the other, seeing that she had tried to save him from going over too soon.

August 18

I saw him again and we went to Graceland. I saw the red couch that I have seen before up in his bedroom, the spread on his bed is red and gold and the toilet is brown and gold, he has a closet the size of a small room with many hats and shoes. We went outside and back around the cars. He wanted to show me his Stutz Blackhawk. I sat on the passenger's side and behind the wheel. The exterior is black with fine walnut grain. I loved it. We walked around outside for a while, he wanted to go down by the horses but I didn't because I said I didn't have any shoes on. He just laughed. He does that a lot. I have seen some pictures of the interior of his house but not the things I have just mentioned. I have also recently seen a picture of his grandmother's nurse and this confirms the lady I saw the night we ran into his grandmother.

August 21

Something happened last night that doesn't make sense, but I'll tell you anyway. I crossed over with El last night. We walked for a while and the area seemed very barren. There was a small canyon which we climbed down and up again. I asked where we were going. We were standing at the top of a hill and down below was a small town. He said I thought you would like to see Iowa. I said why would I want to do that. I really don't want to, he said all right, and we walked back. With that I think I drifted off but woke with a start about two hours later.

August 22
Something clicked in my head this morning and I remembered something that happened last night, either I dreamed it or was told, I don't know. Someone said it was my fault that *Jessie, Elvis's twin, was dead at birth,* that I changed my mind at the last minute and did not want to be a male and that I waited a second too long. I remember I said that you can't lay that guilt on me. That is all that I remember.

Do you remember me telling you that I had the urge to travel, that I wanted to see different things. I just found out that Elvis had planned a European tour to see countries he had never seen. As for Vegas, I found I was taking a lot of his emotions about certain things and places. Dr. Holzer, remind me to tell you about the Roman ruins and the two dead soldiers. I don't know if it is anything, that is why I am not writing it in detail plus I am not sure if this was a dream or a genuine thing.

August 24
When I saw him tonight the only thing I remember is that this time he had on a necklace, a gold one with some kind of medallion or medal. This is the first time he ever wore jewelry. It is reported in some paper that Elvis had a television over his bed. I saw three of them.

Wednesday evening I was having an argument with my husband over my checking account. I was just letting him yell which I do a lot lately; well, anyway I felt the heat starting from my head down until it encompassed my whole body. I then heard El ask what was going on here, I told him not to worry. He asked if I was sure. I said yes. With that, the heat pulled off to the right.

August 25
Elvis wants this book because he wants people to come out of the darkness into the light, and if only a handful accomplish that, the book will be a success. Elvis told me this last night. He also told me that he doesn't write music, but if you just leave yourself open, he will try and help. But just remember, he comes from Gospel roots. I must tell you about the dream that I had after I went to bed and what happened Friday night. Don't forget about this morning at five *A.M.*

August 27
Saw him last night. We walked for a while in a meadow and then around by the lake. We talked for a while to a woman with red hair. She told us everyone knew about us. That they don't make mistakes often and that they always try to correct it and that they are keeping a very close eye on us. We walked some more and then went into a tunnel. When we came out we were riding in a horse and wagon on our way into a town, a very small town about a block long. I actually felt the wagon, the feel of the ride. Elvis didn't look himself, but I knew it was him. He had a haircut like someone had put a bowl on his head and just cut around it. I didn't look like me either. I was very short and wore a kind of drab shirtwaist long dress and a bonnet on my head. I knew we weren't married yet but would be soon. I also knew that he was my brother Zachary's friend and that he lived on the next farm. My daddy always said that I could run the farm better than

Zach because he was a daydreamer. The name of the town was Greenfield or Greensborough or Green Springs, I'm not sure, but I think it has to do with the life in Kentucky. He dropped me off at the general store, which was owned by a Mr. Wilks or Wilkson, I'm not sure of that either. I know I bought some material, one in a print and the other in a heavy denim for Zach's coveralls. I also bought flour and honey and a fancy ribbon which I knew was something important but I don't know what. I left the store and walked down to where Elvis was loading grain or feed. With that we came back to my living room. I was really exhausted. When I come back from any of these trips I can't lift even my arm, everything feels like it weighs a ton.

[There is a Greenville and a Greensborough, Kentucky, both of them very small towns, with a population of less than four thousand inhabitants each. It is unlikely that anyone would know of these towns unless one were actually familiar with them in some way.]

August 29
Saw him briefly, it was a very strange trip. We started out in the park or meadow, and suddenly up onto a road that appeared to be like a gold color, it was very bright. It went up and then it opened up into a round platform with four roads branching off from it. We proceeded to take one and headed down again. We ended up in my living room *looking at my body*. Nothing was said the whole time. He just held my hand the whole time. I have no idea where or what that was.

September 4
I have been having trouble again, contact very poor. *Crossed over a bridge* that spanned a wide gorge that

seemed to have no bottom. We entered a group of trees, then crossed over a hill. We came upon a mass of people, so many that it looked like a sea. There was one man talking and you could hear him as if he was standing next to you. I couldn't make him out too well because he was too far away but he was talking about love and peace and sharing. I heard the whole thing but as soon as I came back I forgot most of it. I'm sorry. Returned through a tunnel, as usual.

September 10
We were standing on a hill looking down at a very large group of people who were lined up in four different lines which were very long. *Walking up and down these lines were men with large books,* stopping once in a while and talking to some of the people on line. There were paths stretching out to what seemed to be space going in all different directions. Elvis told me these people were coming back. I remember saying that you will have to stand on line to come back and after that I remember nothing. I woke or came back about two hours later, feeling very heavy and sick. I went to stand up, and my legs gave way.

Dorothy Sherry's mother, herself psychic since childhood, was able to contribute some important material to my research, both as an observer of her daughter's behavior and experiences, sometimes as a witness to them, and, as I will show, as a direct psychic contact for Elvis Presley at times when Elvis made no effort to conceal his presence in Dorothy's house. Mrs. T., Dorothy's mother, who usually accompanied her daughter when Dorothy Sherry visited me at my study in New York City, was the first one to

hear about her daughter's unusual visit to Las Vegas. Although the family stayed at another hotel, Dorothy
couldn't wait to get over to the Hilton Hotel, inspired by
her unseen companion, Elvis Presley—unseen, that is, to
everyone but herself. Here is the report by Mrs. T., written down immediately upon her daughter's return, when
the memory of what had transpired in Las Vegas was still
fresh.

July 31
Dorothy came home from Vegas all excited. All the
things she was seeing in real life were the things he had
shown her so often before. Elvis was with her all the
time and as Dorothy walked into the Hilton she could
hear him say, home at last. Boy, she said, she felt wonderful. Her sister-in-law who was with her wanted the
ladies' room and Dorothy directed her to it like an old
pro. Dorothy also saw a gift shop where Elvis had
bought a nightgown and robe for some girl and another
gift shop where he said he had bought a ring and a few
other things. Dorothy said she was taking on some of
his depressed feelings and some of his happiness feelings
at times. She also told me she saw how Elvis was lying
when he was dead. She said that half his face was into
the rug and that one hand was extended, sort of up-
ward. It was hard for me to talk to her as her husband
was in and out of her room. She told me once more
that on leaving the Hilton Elvis was depressed, I think
that is when he came to *me* crying.

As you know I have seen him in her home and also in
my home and that is why I don't doubt that what is
happening is real. At first I was very upset. And when
she told me in January 1978 it was hard to take, and I

thought she was losing her mind, as a thing like this had never happened to her before. That is why I asked our mutual friend to contact you for us, as I knew that you are known in this area and that you would be able to tell us if my daughter needed any sort of psychiatric help or not.

While Dorothy was on vacation in Las Vegas, I was looking at television one evening when all of a sudden I saw Elvis. He was sweating and crying. I said to him, just what are you doing here? I am not going to wipe away your tears, you are supposed to be with my daughter Dorothy, you said you were going to show her a good time, get back to her and make sure she's all right. He gave me that wink of his and left. I always send him to her when I see him as I feel she's safe with him by her side. He has told me never to doubt that he would look after her and make sure she's all right. Last night he said, "What about that book?" I told him we were working on it. [At the time this letter was written and mailed, *no plans for a book* had as yet been formulated in my mind, nor had I agreed to do a book.]

The night that Dorothy came home, she and Elvis went to visit a friend, also named Dorothy, who happened to be in the hospital. My daughter Dorothy told me that the woman was in a bed near a window with her hair piled up in a bun, and nearby was a nightstand with some odds and ends on it, which my daughter Dorothy also described in detail. Today we called the woman in question and checked it out: it was perfectly true what my daughter had seen in the astral state.

I next had occasion to question Dorothy's mother on September 12, 1978, when she stated that my article for the *National Enquirer* would be available on the following Saturday. It was, and her intuition was indeed amazing because I had no idea on what day the newspaper would eventually publish the story. While driving home from the place where she had picked up the newspaper and with her hands on the wheel she felt two arms being put around her and holding her. They were unseen arms, and she knew they belonged to Elvis Presley. I questioned her about the incident. Here is her own statement.

"As we came in from buying the paper and walked into the house, both of us saw a man standing there. I yelled that there was a burglar in the house. The man had on black slacks and a white shirt. Quick as a flash he was gone."

After that, I heard nothing from Dorothy for a long time. But suddenly, she was on the telephone again: could she come and see me right away? Elvis was back.

When I saw her, she slipped into a trance quite readily. "Mr. Presley," as I always called "him" in this situation, wanted me to write a memorial album of songs expressing his philosophy about life after death and reincarnation. I replied that I was not much of a rock 'n' roll writer, though I do have a background in popular music. Somewhat annoyed, Elvis replied, "Don't you know I've also had two albums of spiritual songs?"

I didn't. But I went ahead anyway and started to write down those songs. In the midst of it, I halted and asked Dorothy to return.

"Look," I said to Elvis via his entranced medium, "I can't go on writing these songs if I don't know who will ever record them . . . and that is, after all, what you want."

There was a moment of *dead* silence. Then the communicator snorted—"Pickwick. Go to Pickwick!" And he was gone, and Dorothy woke up.

I found Pickwick Records in the New York telephone book. No, they had never had any dealing with Elvis. I was about to put down the telephone, when the man at Pickwick added, "—but there is another Pickwick Records in Minneapolis. Try that." I did.

Did they have any connection with Elvis Presley? They did indeed.

"We produced his two albums of spiritual songs," the Minneapolis Pickwick man said. Now could the medium have known *that*? She couldn't have.

Hopefully, the album and the story of Elvis and Dorothy—the only true evidential contact with the postmortem Elvis—will eventually be public knowledge.

I rest my case.

What remains to be addressed with respect to all I now know about Elvis Presley, his life, and, ah yes, his afterlife, is perhaps a bit anticlimatic. I know why he picked Dorothy to be his "mouthpiece"—a very unlikely one, who at the time of her first trance was certainly innocent of any and all privy knowledge about him, and was in no way a professional psychic. Years later, Dorothy, divorced by then, turned to giving simple readings in a New Jersey shopping mall to make ends meet. Even today she is not exactly famous as a psychic.

I also know why Elvis chose me to be his voice to the wider world. He did have some of my books and he did have an active interest in the paranormal and spiritual. He was right in turning to me—both a convinced advocate for life beyond physical death on a purely empiric, scientific basis, and a properly trained academic investigator.

Each year when the anniversary of Elvis's death or his birthday comes around, the days are marked internationally with increasing fervor and devotion by his millions of faithful fans. Death has not changed that; to the contrary, it has made the bonds even stronger. The question then is why. Who really is Elvis? The living Elvis appealed, I think, to a part of our soul frequently left unsatisfied. It is not a great secret that the majority of people in all walks of life are less than totally happy in their emotional lives. Yet society marches on, accepting partial satisfaction of our basic desire for emotional fulfillment as the norm to be attained. It has to—otherwise few relationships would occur.

Elvis, like the classical gods of antiquity, blended an attractive physical appearance, a voice filled with emotion and feeling, and a certain animal magnetism into a true triune personality of body, mind, and spirit.

To the women in his audience—his fans, his admirers— he was a Greek god who supplied what their human male companions could not. To his male admirers, he represented the total goal, to be like him, to improve one's own person to match his. This is not necessarily a sexual appeal per se; it runs much deeper, probably largely on the unconscious level. To the people of antiquity, all this was simple and clear. The gods came down from Mount Olympus and mingled with mortals to have fun, making the mortals happy, if only temporarily, and to beget children who, being partly of divine origin, would turn out to be larger than mortal life.

Modern man does not have the luxury of Greek mythology, and perhaps not even the reassurance of Freudian or

Jungian psychiatry. But the reactions are quite the same as they were three thousand years ago.

Elvis's medium was music and artistry, the most direct and most universal way to reach the masses, if his message was to be heard, and perhaps understood and implemented. It is no accident that with all the worldly trappings of his life, with all his trespasses as a human being, Elvis early on tended to include the Spiritual Path of Understanding in his way of life. God's ways are strange at times, but always purposeful. To place an Elvis into this world of imperfection and destructiveness was truly worthy of the Deity.

I can only hope that Elvis Presley's message from the Other Side of Life, over there and yet so near, will reach all of us sooner or later.

Jean Harlow's *Restless Spirit*

If any movie actress deserved the name of "vamp," it certainly was Jean Harlow. The blonde actress personified the ideal of the 1930s— slim and sultry, moving her body in a provocative manner, dressing in the rather elegant, seemingly casual style of that period. Slinky dresses, sweaters, and colorful accessories made Jean Harlow one of the outstanding glamour girls of the American screen. The public was never let in on any of her personal secrets or, for that matter, her personal tragedies. Her life story was carefully edited to present only those aspects of her personality that fitted in with the preconceived notion of what a glamorous movie star should be like. In a way, Jean Harlow was the prototype of all later blonde bombshells of the screen, culminating with the late Marilyn Monroe. There is a striking parallel, too, in the tragic lives and sometimes ends of these blonde movie queens. Quite possibly the image they projected on the screen, or were forced to project, was at variance with their own private achievements and helped pave the way to their tragic downfalls.

To me, Jean Harlow will always stand out as the glamorous goddess of such motion pictures as *Red Dust*, which I saw as a little boy. The idea that she could have had an earthbound life after death seems to be very far from the image the actress portrayed during her lifetime. Thus it was with some doubt that I followed up a lead supplied by an English newspaper, which said the former home of the screen star was haunted.

The house in question is a handsome white stucco one-family house set back somewhat from a quiet residential street in Westwood, a section of Los Angeles near the university generally considered quiet and upper middle class. The house itself belongs to a professional man and his wife, who share it with their two daughters and two poodles. It is a two-story building with an elegant staircase winding from the rear of the ground floor to the upper story. The downstairs portion contains a rather large oblong living room that leads into a dining room. There are a kitchen and bathroom adjacent to that area and a stairway leading to the upper floor. Upstairs are two bedrooms and a bathroom.

When I first spoke on the telephone to Mrs. H. the present occupant of the house, asking permission to visit, she responded rather cordially. A little later I called back to make a definite appointment and found that her husband was far from pleased with my impending visit. Although he himself had experienced some of the unusual phenomena in the house, as a professional, he was worried that publicity might hurt his career. I assured him that I was not interested in disclosing his name or address, and with that assurance I was again welcomed. It was a sunny afternoon when I picked up my tape recorder and camera, left my taxicab in front of the white house in Westwood, and rang the bell.

Mrs. H. was already expecting me. She turned out to be a petite, dark-blonde lady of around thirty, very much given to conversation and more than somewhat interested in the occult. As a matter of fact, she had read one of my earlier books. With her was a woman friend; whether the friend had been asked out of curiosity or security I do not know. At any rate the three of us sat down in the living room and I started to ask Mrs. H. the kind of questions I always ask when I come to an allegedly haunted house.

"Mrs. H., how long have you lived in this house?"

"Approximately four years."

"When you bought it, did you make any inquiries as to the previous owner?"

"I did not. I didn't really care. I walked into the house and I liked it and that was that."

"Did you just tell your husband to buy it?"

"Yes. I told him, 'This is our house.' I had the realtor go ahead and draw up the papers before he saw it because I knew he would feel as I did."

"Where did you live before?"

"All over—Brentwood, West Los Angeles, Beverly Hills. I was born in Canada."

"How many years have you been married?"

"Seventeen."

"You have children?"

"I have two daughters, nine and twelve."

"Did the real-estate man tell you anything about the house?"

"He did not."

"After you moved in and got settled, did you make some changes in it?"

"Yes; it was in kind of sad shape. It needed somebody to love it."

"Did you make any structural changes?"

"No. When we found out the history of the house we decided we would leave it as it was."

"So at the time you moved in, you just fixed it?"

"Yes."

"When was the first time that you had any *unusual* feelings about the house?"

"The day before we moved in I came over to direct the men who were laying the carpet. I walked upstairs and I had an experience at that time."

"What happened?"

"My two dogs ran barking and growling into the upstairs bedrooms; I went up, and I thought I heard something *whisper in my ear*. It scared me."

"That was in one of the upstairs bedrooms?"

"No, in the hallway just before the master bedroom. The dogs ran in barking and growling as if they were going to get somebody, and then when they got in there they looked around and there was nobody there."

"What did you hear?"

"I could swear I heard somebody say, *'Please help me!'* It was a soft whisper, sort of hushed."

"What did you do?"

"I talked to myself for a few minutes to get my bearings. I had never experienced anything like *that*, and I figured, 'Well, if it's there, fine.' I've had *other* ESP experiences before, so I just went about my business."

"Those other experiences you've had—were they before you came to this house?"

"Yes. I have heard my name being called."

"In this house or in another?"

"In other homes."

"Anyone you could recognize?"

"No, just female voices."

"Did you *see* anything unusual at any time?"

"I saw what I assume to be ectoplasm. . . . It was like cigarette smoke. It moved, and my dogs whined, tucked their tails between their legs, and fled from the room."

"Did you tell your husband about the whisper?"

"I did not. My husband is skeptical. I saw no reason to tell him."

"When was the next time you had any feeling of a presence here?"

"The night we moved in, my husband and I were lying in bed. Suddenly, it was as if the bed were hit by a very strong object three times. My husband said, 'My God, I'm getting out of here. This place is haunted.' I replied, 'Oh, shush. It's all right if someone is trying to communicate. It's not going to hurt.' And to the ghost I said, 'You're welcome—how do you do; but we've got to get some sleep—we're very, very tired—so please let us be.' "

"And did it help?"

"Yes."

"How long did the peace last?"

"Well, the jerking of the bed never happened again. But other things happened. There is a light switch on my oven in the kitchen. For a long time after we moved in, the switch would go on every so often—by itself."

"Would it take anyone to turn it physically, to turn on the light?"

"Yes, you'd have to flip it up."

"Was there anybody else in the house who could have done it?"

"No, because I would be sitting here and I'd hear the click and I would go there and it would be *on*. It's happened ten or fifteen times, but recently it has stopped."

"Any other phenomena?"

"Something new one time, at dusk. I was walking from one room to the other. I was coming through the dining room, and for some reason I looked up at the ceiling. There it was, this light—"

"Did it have any particular shape?"

"No. It moved at the edges, but it really didn't have a form. It wasn't a solid mass, more like an outline. It was floating above me."

"Did you hear anything?"

"Not at that time. I have on one occasion. I was sitting right in the chair I am in now. My Aunt Mary was in that chair, and we both heard *sobs*. Terrible, sad, wrenching sobs coming from the corner over there by the mailbox. It was very upsetting, to say the least."

"Were these a woman's sobs?"

"Definitely."

"Did you see anything at the time?"

"No. I just felt terribly sad, and the hair stood up on my arms. Also, in this house there are *winds* at times, when there is no window open."

"Are there any cold spots that cannot be explained rationally?"

"Very frequently. Downstairs, usually here or in the upstairs bedroom, sometimes also in the kitchen."

"At the time your Aunt Mary was sitting here and you heard the sobs, did she also hear them?"

"Oh, she did, and I had to give her a drink."

"Have you heard any other sounds?"

"Footsteps. Up and down the stairs when nobody was walking up or down."

"Male or female?"

"I would say female, because they are light. I have also felt things brush by my face, touching my cheek."

"Since you came to this home, have you had any unusual dreams?"

"Definitely. One very important one. I was in bed and just dozing off, when I had a vision. I saw very vividly a picture of the upstairs bathroom. I saw a hand reaching out of a bathtub full of water, going up to the light switch, the socket where you turn power on and off. It then turned into a vision of wires, and brisk voltage struck the hand; the hand withered and died. It upset me terribly. The next morning my husband said, 'You know, I had the strangest dream last night.' He had had the *identical dream!*"

"Identical?"

"Practically. In his version, the hand didn't wither, but he saw the sparks coming out of it. I went into the bathroom and decided to call in an electrician. He took out the outdated switch. He said, 'Did you know this is outlawed? If anybody had been in the tub and reached up and touched the switch, he would have been electrocuted!' We moved the switch so the only way you can turn the switch on is *before* you go into the bathroom. You can no longer reach it from the tub. Whoever helped me with this—I'm terribly grateful to her."

"Is there anything else of this kind you would care to tell me?"

"I have smelled perfume in the upstairs children's bedroom, a very strong perfume. I walked into the room. My little daughter who sleeps there doesn't have perfume. That's the only place I smell it, my little girl's bedroom."

"Has any visitor ever come to this house without knowledge of the phenomena and complained about anything unusual?"

"A friend named Betty sat in the kitchen and said, 'My gosh, I wish you'd close the windows. There's such a draft in here.' But everything was shut tight."

"Has your husband observed anything unusual except for the dream?"

"One evening in the bedroom he said, 'Boy, there's a draft in here!' I said there couldn't be. All the windows were closed."

"What about the children?"

"My youngest daughter, Jenny, has complained she hears a party in her upstairs closet. She says that people are having a party in it. She can hear them."

"When was the house built?"

"I believe in 1929."

"Was it built to order for anyone?"

"No. It was just built like many houses in this area, and then put up for sale."

"Who was the first tenant here?"

"It was during the Depression. There were several successive tenants."

"How did Jean Harlow get involved with the house?"

"She was living in a small home, but the studio told her she should live in a better area. She rented this house in the early '30s and moved into it with her parents."

"How long did she live here?"

"About four years. She paid the rent on it longer, however, because after she married, her folks stayed in this house. I believe she married her agent."

"How did she die?"

"She died, I understand, as the result of a beating given to her by her husband which damaged her kidneys. The story goes that on the second night, after their honeymoon, he beat her. She came back to this house, took her mother into the bathroom and showed her what he had done to her. She was covered with bruises. She tried to make up with him, but to no avail. The night he killed himself, she was in this house. There was a rumor that he was impotent or a latent homosexual. He shot himself. When she heard the news, she was in her upstairs bedroom. She tried to commit suicide, because she thought she was the reason. She took an overdose of sleeping pills."

"Did she succeed?"

"She did not. Her parents put pressure on her to move out of this house. She built another one and subsequently died of a kidney disease."

"Not immediately after the beating?"

"No—a few years later. Her parents were Christian Scientists, and she didn't have ordinary medical help at the time."

"Then what took place in this house, emotionally speaking? The marriage to Paul Bern, the news of his suicide, and her own attempt to commit suicide upstairs. Which rooms were particularly connected with these events?"

"The living room. She was married there. And the bathroom upstairs. I left it as it was."

"Do you have any feelings about it?"

"I have a feeling about the bathroom. I know she's been in that bathroom many times. I don't know if she tried to commit suicide in the bathroom or if she took the pills in the bedroom."

"Where did the actual beating take place?"

"They say it was in the bathroom downstairs."

"Which is the bathroom you have such a weird feeling in, the downstairs or the upstairs?"

"Downstairs."

"Anything pertaining to the front or the outside of the house?"

"There are knocks at our front door when there is nobody there; visitors would say, 'There's someone at your door,' and there wasn't. . . . It happens all the time."

"Are you sure other people hear the knocks too?"

"Yes."

"Somebody couldn't have done it and run away in a hurry?"

"No. It's a funny knock. Kind of gentle. It isn't like a 'let-me-in' type knock. Flesh-and-blood people wouldn't knock on a door that way."

"When was the last time you had any feeling of a presence in this house?"

"Maybe two or three months ago."

"Do you feel she's still around?"

"Yes. Also, I feel she was very upset at the way she was portrayed as a kind of loose woman without morals. Her biography presents her as something she was not."

"Do you think she's trying to express herself through you?"

"No, but I think it's terrible what they've done to her reputation. They had no right to do that."

"Do you feel that she's trying to set the record straight?"

"I would imagine. I can only put myself in her place. If I were to cross over under those circumstances, I would be very unhappy. I hope some day somebody will write another book about Harlow and go into it with a sensitive, loving attitude instead of sensationalism as a way to make a fast buck."

I thanked Mrs. H. and prepared to leave the house that had once been Jean Harlow's. Perhaps the lady of the house was merely reliving the more emotional aspects of the late screen star's life, the way an old film is rerun from time to time on television. Was she picking up these vibrations from the past through psychometry? Or was there perhaps something of the *substance* of Jean Harlow still present in the atmosphere of this house? As I walked out the front door into the still-warm late afternoon, I looked back at Mrs. H., who stood in the doorway waving me good-bye. Her blonde hair was framed by the shadow cast by the door itself. For a fleeting moment, some of the blonde glamour of the late Jean Harlow seemed to have impressed itself upon her face. Perhaps it was only my imagination, but all of a sudden I felt that Jean Harlow hadn't really left the house where so much of her emotional life had taken place.

The Troubled Ghost
of Carole Lombard

I was in San Diego, California, doing a local television show to discuss one of my books. A fellow guest was an attractive young lady who had had some psychic experiences, so the producer thought that putting us together on this show was a stroke of genius. It turned out to be more than that: it was the hand of fate. A close friendship of many years' standing and many exciting adventures into the so-called supernatural were the result of this "chance" meeting. I was asked to interview the young lady on the show, and I did. We hit it off right away. That is how I met Julie Parrish for the first time.

Julie was then appearing in a daytime serial called "Good Morning, World." She had done numerous stints on television shows and appeared in several motion pictures. In retrospect I find it ironic that she appeared in *Harlow* for Paramount. But the subject that intrigued Julie most at that time was not so much how to get a good role in another movie as how to understand herself and her strange psychic abilities. In the five years that I have known Julie she has come a long way. She has been a professional astrologer whose predictions I have quoted liberally in a book called *The Prophets Speak,* and she has been a psychic whose extraordinary sensitivity was recorded by Jess Stearn in one of his earlier works. She became one of the stars of the revived series "Peyton Place" and leads a very busy life that doesn't permit her as much psychic activity as she might like. It was all there in her "chart" several years ago, so she is quite content to let fate take a hand in her life and simply wait to see what happens.

Julie Parrish is five feet five, with dark-blonde hair that from time to time turns brown, hazel eyes, and a slim figure. At that time she looked about twenty-two, and now, five years later, she looks about twenty-three. This is due not to any miracle but to her deep understanding of Yoga, her diet of health foods, and her observance of the rhythm of proper living, all of which allow her to replenish her depleted energies even after doing one television show a day, five days a week, year in and year out. Julie is an advanced soul in the esoteric sense. She has read a great deal and met many people in the esoteric field who have taught her some of the fundamentals of balancing body, mind, and spirit in daily living. All this has not materially advanced her career, but it has made her into a very strong person, able to cope with the stress of a Hollywood career under conditions that might make weaker individuals falter.

In 1961 Julie was living in Toledo, Ohio, sharing an apartment on Collingwood Boulevard with two roommates. It was a very well preserved old house; the girls' apartment was a huge one that took up the entire top floor. On this particular day she found herself all alone recuperating from a cold. As she lay in bed she gradually slipped into that state between wakefulness and sleep in which psychic experiences frequently occur. As she did so, she became aware of a lady all dressed in black, wearing a mourning veil and hat, standing in the doorway. Julie could not see her face well, but the woman looked at her and then slowly crossed to the closet on her right and looked inside. Petrified, Julie watched her without moving. She tried to scream, but no sound came. The woman then turned and walked toward the bed. In panic, Julie closed her eyes. The woman moved closer and bent down to her, and Julie could actually feel her breath on her face. It was as though she were taking her breath away. With all the strength Julie could muster, she burst out of the trance state, and as she did, the woman disappeared.

After Julie had moved to Los Angeles, she lived in an old house built in the thirties by the late Wilfred Orme of the Warner Bros. art department. There she spent four and a half years. During that time she had many psychic experiences—people running around and slamming doors, loud footsteps, inaudible conversations. Whenever she checked she would find that no one was there. These manifestations always took place during the daytime, when she could have seen plainly whether there was really anyone there or not. Strangely, they took place only when Julie was in that state between wakefulness and sleep where physical responses are low yet attention is still riveted on anything unusual around oneself. The large number of these psychic experiences so unnerved her that she put aluminum foil on her bedroom windows, so that whenever she rested, no light would come in through the windows and send her into the astral state.

Several times Julie felt that someone unseen was trying to smother her. Each time the experience threw her into a panic. Eventually she investigated the background of the house and discovered that a man had killed himself in it. The only nonthreatening feature of her experiences in the house was that when she was in the psychic state she could hear the radio playing beside her bed even though it was not turned on. When in her normal state of wakefulness she turned the radio on, she would discover that it was broadcasting the music she had heard in her head while in the psychic state.

In the late sixties she went to Las Vegas on business. It was a dark afternoon in November when she registered at the Sands Hotel and checked into room 1888. Tired from the trip and from a long evening the night before, she went to bed, hoping to sleep late the next day. Thus it was already well into that day when she awoke. What broke her sleep was not the lateness of the hour, however, but the laughing and the loud conversation of three men and two women sitting and standing in various positions around a table at the foot of her bed. Julie immediately sensed that they were not exactly "nice people." They stared at her, and she felt embarrassed, since she wasn't wearing much because of the warmth of the room. A man on the right turned to the others and said, "What should we do with her?"

This abruptly brought her back to her conscious state. She realized then that she had seen the ghosts of five people who had been killed in the immediate vicinity and who had for some reason chosen her room to go over old memories.

Late in 1969 Julie moved to New York for a while and decided to work with me in perfecting her control over the psychic talent she so amply possessed. We used hypnosis to widen her psychic perception, and eventually I tested her in various ways to determine how much her psychometry had grown as a result of our working together. Among other things, I tested her with letters written by various people whom I knew but of whom Julie knew nothing. She was quite remarkable with a note from the late Bishop James Pike and with another letter written by a late friend of mine, Dr. Thomas Mabbott, professor of English at Hunter College. In each case she characterized the writer quite accurately, even though she could not have deduced anything from the writing itself or the contents. But it was in October of the following year, in Hollywood, that Julie and I worked on our most interesting case together.

In 1967 I first heard of a haunted house where the late Carole Lombard had lived. During a séance in Greenwich Village, I heard of a Mexican-born lady named Adriana de Sola who had been to the Village flat and had seen a ghost in it, and I became interested in meeting her. Some time later I did meet her in Hollywood. Miss de Sola was by vocation a poet and writer, but she made her living in various ways, usually as a housekeeper. In the late forties she had been engaged as such by a motion picture producer of some renown. She supervised the staff, a job she performed very well indeed, being an excellent organizer. Carefully inspecting the house before agreeing to take the position, she had found it one of those quiet, elegant houses in the best part of Hollywood that could harbor nothing but good. Confidently, Adriana had taken the job.

A day or two after her arrival, she was fast asleep in her room when she found herself aroused in the middle of the night by someone shaking her. Fully awake, she realized that she was being shaken by the shoulder. She sat up in bed, but there was no one to be seen. Even though she could not with her ordinary sight distinguish any human being in the room, her psychic sense told her immediately that there was someone standing next to her bed. Relaxing for a moment and closing her eyes, Adriana tried to tune in on the unseen entity. Immediately she saw, standing next to her bed, a tall, slim woman with blonde hair down to her shoulders. What made the apparition or psychic impression the more upsetting to Adriana was the fact that the woman was bathed in blood and quite obviously suffering.

Adriana realized that she had been contacted by a ghostly entity but could not get herself to accept the reality of the phenomenon, and ascribed it hopefully to an upset stomach, or to the new surroundings and the upsets of having just moved in. At the same time, she prayed for the restless one. But six or seven days later the same thing happened again. This time Adriana was able to see the ghost more clearly. She was impressed with the great beauty of the woman she saw and decided to talk about her experience with her employers in the morning. The producer's wife listened very quietly to the description of the ghostly visitor, then nodded. When Adriana mentioned that the apparition had been wearing a light suit covered with blood, the lady of the house drew back in surprise. It was only then that Adriana learned that the house had once been Carole Lombard's and that the late movie star had lived in it very happily with Clark Gable. Carole Lombard had died tragically in an airplane accident, when her plane, en route to the East where she was going to do some USO shows, hit a mountain during a storm. At the time, she was wearing a light-colored suit.

Miss de Sola was pleased, in a way, that her psychic ability had been proved correct. At the same time, she realized that the two visits by the restless one were not going to be the only ones, and she was not prepared to open herself up to further visitations. Two days later she regretfully informed her employers that she could not stay on after all.

Many years later Julie Parrish asked me to look into a case of some interest brought to her attention by a doctor friend of hers named Doris August. The doctor had a house in Hollywood where some disturbances of a psychic nature had occurred. Would I follow through?

The house, an older wooden structure set back a bit from the street in a quiet section of Hollywood, turned out to be the former home of the motion picture producer who had tried to employ Miss de Sola. Since then several owners had come and gone in rapid succession. The doctor felt quite comfortable in it, and the feeling of a presence had not in the least disturbed her, especially as she was convinced of the reality of psychic phenomena. We did not discuss anything about the house at first, but I asked Julie to move about the two floors to see whether she could pick up anything unusual in a psychic sense, and also to feel out the house for any actual presences that might have remained in the atmosphere. After a while she stretched out on a couch in the living room and I placed her into light trance. We lowered the lights, closed the windows and the door, and waited quietly for what might come through Julie's lips, or for that matter what might happen to us. The only other person present was Dr. August.

For the first five or six minutes there was absolutely nothing. I decided to start by addressing myself to the unseen entity or entities present. I realized, of course, that Julie knew that the house had once belonged to Carole Lombard, as did I. Beyond this fact, however, no details were known to either of us. Anything Dr. August might tell us would have to be discussed after the attempt to make contact with the entity in the house.

The traffic on Sunset Boulevard, a few yards away, seemed strangely muted at this moment, and I had the distinct feeling that we were back in the thirties. The atmosphere of the house felt musty and contained, as if time had stood still and we had stepped into a time lock of sorts. I looked toward the handsome bar in the corner of the room, for no particular reason, and then addressed myself to parties unknown.

"If there is anyone present who wishes to communicate with us, let him speak through Julie. We have come as friends, to set things right, to help if we can. Julie, do you see anyone present in this atmosphere?"

"There's a woman here, but she's laughing at you. She doesn't understand what it is you're doing and why."

"What does she look like?"

"She has on a red dress, and she's a blonde. She doesn't know what you're doing here."

"I'm here to help her make contact. Does she seem young or old?"

"She's young."

"Is she hurt in any way?"

"She seems fine, but *I* don't feel well."

"What do you feel?"

"I feel very hot; my head is hurting, and my throat hurts. I think this is something that she's showing me *she* feels."

"Ask her to identify herself by name."

"What is your name? . . . Her name is Carole."

"Is this her house?"

"Yes."

"Does she remember passing over? Dying?"

"She doesn't know that she's dead."

"Does she remember a plane ride she took many years ago?"

"Yes, she does."

"Does she remember being in that airplane?"

"She seems confused."

"Is there anyone she wants to find?"

"She's looking for Clark. She came back and he didn't recognize her; she tried to talk to him and he couldn't talk to her; he couldn't see her. And now she can't find him. She wants very much to find him because she wants to tell him that she's sorry, that she loves him very much. But he couldn't hear her."

"Where did she try to talk to him?"

"I don't know. She's feeling these things."

"All right, we will help her. Ask her to listen very carefully."

(In a whisper) "Okay."

"Carole, you were in a plane accident. The plane crashed. You were killed. Your spirit survived. You came back to your house, but no one could see or hear you because you were a spirit and they were not psychic enough to understand this. Does she understand?"

"She's very quiet."

"You have passed over into the next stage of life. You are very much alive, but out of the physical body. You are a spirit. But this must not upset you. Clark has been over some years too. You are both on the same side, and you could get together if you wished. Does she wish to find Clark?"

"Yes."

"She must call out to him. First she must understand that she has passed over and is no longer in the physical world. Does she understand that?"

"She's trying to."

"Tell her she must not hold onto this house which is *not* of the spirit world; the moment she relinquishes her attachment to this house, she will be free to find him."

"She says it's her house, but things have changed."

"Does she wish to join Clark? I will tell her what she must do."

"She hears you."

"Call for Clark to take you away from this house, to *his* house, and he will come for you. That is all that is necessary. But she must do it of her own volition. Is she doing it?"

"Well, she hesitates."

"Why is she hesitating?"

"Is there a—a Mrs.—Reade—R-e-d-e—"

"Who is Mrs. Rede?"

"A dressmaker!"

"What about her?"

"She has—the jewelry. She has the earrings."

"What does she want done with them?"

"She just wants to tell you. She left it there. She took it off and threw it there."

"Is it all right with her that Mrs. Rede has her jewelry?"

"It's not there anymore; she only wanted you to know where it was, at the time. People were looking."

"Does she remember the accident?"

"She was very frightened."

"Tell her she's fine now, and fully alive. Tell her to begin by calling for Clark."

"She's using her mind."

"I ask that this entity be helped across, to relinquish all ties with this house and earth, and to be taken in hand by the one she seeks. I ask that my friends on the other side actively assist her in crossing. Carole, go from this place; do not look back upon it; keep it in your memories, but go on to better things, and above all, go on to join your loved one. He awaits you."

"Yes. She understands."

"I send you away from this house, Carole, into the next stage of life where you will find Clark if you desire. I send you away from the earth plane. Go now."

"She's not here anymore."

A moment later Julie Parrish was back to herself. Shaking off the sleeplike trance, she sat up and spoke to me about the experience of the last few minutes. She remembered most of it, although not everything. Since the trance had been a light one, that was to be expected. Immediately I questioned Julie about her conscious memories of the encounter with the entity in this house, before she could forget it or before discussion could add details which were not originally in her mind. What exactly did she recall?

"I saw a blonde lady."

"What kind of a dress did she wear?"

"Red. She was slim, very pretty, and had blue eyes."

"Hair?"

"Short, kind of curly."

"Anything else about her?"

"She seemed confused. As if she were in limbo."

"How do you yourself feel?"

"Fine."

I now turned to the owner of the house. "Dr. August, how long have you been in this house?"

"Twenty years."

"Have you ever experienced anything unusual?"

"No."

"Has anyone else?"

"They say they have. Kenny Kingston, the psychic, came here six months ago. He and a number of friends wanted to have a séance."

"But did anyone have any experiences prior to that?"

"No, but they knew it was Carole Lombard's house and they wanted to try."

"What happened during the séance?"

"They said they saw her. She came into the room with flowers and seemed very happy."

"How was she described?"

"Very slender; had her hair kind of loose, and she was wearing a red dress."

"How many people saw her?"

"The whole group—there were about thirty—said that they did."

"Dr. August, do you have any comments on the material we have just obtained with Julie?"

"Only this: On the night Kenny Kingston was here with his group, he told us there had been a big fight between Clark and Carole, just before she left on her fatal journey."

The entranced Julie had spoken of a tearful Carole asking forgiveness from her Clark. Julie had no way of knowing either about the quarrel just prior to Carole Lombard's last flight or that she had been seen by others in the house prior to her visit wearing the identical red dress Julie had seen her in. Perhaps a lover's quarrel and a red dress aren't much in the way of psychic evidence, as evidence goes. But psychic researchers must attach comparatively great importance to minor details, because only thus are they able to come to any kind of conclusion when dealing with the ghosts of well-known personalities. The press may have published much about the major aspects of Carole Lombard's life, but I doubt that they printed any report of a lover's quarrel just before her departure for New York, or mentioned anything about a red dress.

Hanging Out
with the Late Barrymores

Paula Davidson is a charming, introspective girl from Cleveland, Ohio, who decided that a career in the entertainment field could be best achieved by moving to Los Angeles. In 1969 she arrived in Beverly Hills and took a job with a major advertising agency. The job was fine, but there was something peculiar about the house into which she had moved. In the first place, it was far too large to be a one-family home, and yet she had been told that it once belonged to one family —the family of Lionel Barrymore. Perched high in the Hollywood hills, the house gives a deceptive impression if one approaches it from the street. From that side it presents only two stories, but the rear of the house looks down into a deep ravine, perhaps as much as five or six stories deep. There is even a private cable car, no longer in use. The once beautiful gardens have long since fallen into disrepair and now present a picture of sad neglect.

On the whole, the house was and is the kind of palatial

mansion a Barrymore would have felt at home in. Although the gardens have been neglected for years, the house itself is still bright, having been painted recently, and its Spanish décor adds to the mystique of its background. When Paula Davidson took up residence there, the owner had been forced to sublet part of the house for financial reasons. One of the rooms in what used to be the former servants' quarters was rented to Heidi, a composer who wrote musical scores for films. She was in the habit of practicing in the music room on the first level. Heidi liked to practice during the day, since everyone else was at work and the house was quiet. In the stillness of the empty house she would frequently hear footsteps approaching as if someone unseen were listening to her playing. On one occasion she clearly heard a baby cry when there was no baby in the house.

I promised Paula I would look into the matter, and on May 31, 1969, she picked me up at the Continental Hotel to take me to the Barrymore mansion. With us was another friend named Jill Taggart, who had worked with me before. A writer and sometime model, Jill had displayed ESP talents at an early age and shown amazing abilities with clairvoyance and psychometry. It occurred to me that taking her to a place she knew nothing about, without telling her where we were going and why, might yield some interesting results. Consequently I avoided discussing anything connected with the purpose of our visit.

When we arrived at the mansion, the owner of the house greeted us cordially. Paula, Heidi, the owner, and I started out following Jill around the house as my psychic friend tried to get her bearings. Unfortunately, however, we had picked an evening when some of the other tenants in the house were having a party. What greeted us on our arrival was not the serene stillness of a night in the Hollywood hills but the overly loud blaring of a jukebox and the stamping of many feet in one of the basement rooms.

I have never worked under worse conditions. Under the circumstances, however, we had no choice but to try to get whatever we could. Even before we entered the house Jill remarked that she felt two people, a man and a woman, hanging on in the atmosphere, and she had the feeling that someone was watching us. Then she added, "She died a long time after he did." I questioned her further about the entities she felt present. "She's old; he's young. He must have been in his thirties; she is considerably older. I get the feeling of him as a memory. Perhaps only her memory of him, but whichever one of the entities is here, it is madder than hell at the moment." With the noise of the music going on downstairs I couldn't rightly blame the ghost for being mad. Jill then pointed at a corner of the house and said, "I keep seeing the corner of the house up there."

I later discovered that the top room was a kind of ballroom with a balcony. In it Heidi frequently heard a telephone ring, but that was not the only part of the house where an invisible telephone kept ringing. "I used to be down in the bottom room, the one right next to where the noise is now," Heidi explained, "practicing my music, but I'd constantly have to stop, thinking I heard the telephone ring. Of course there was no telephone." I took Heidi aside so that Jill could not hear her remarks. Jill would not have been interested anyway, for she was engrossed in her study of the house now, walking up and down the stairs, peering into rooms with a quizzical expression on her face.

"Tell me," I asked Heidi, "what else did you experience in this house?"

"Frequently when I was down in that room playing the piano I would hear people walking on the stairs; this happened at all times of the day, and there was never anyone up there."

Jill was passing by us now. "I picked up a name," she said. "Grace—and then there is something that sounds like Hugen." I looked at the owner of the house. Jill was out of earshot again. "The party who had the house before us was Arty Erin," the owner said, shrugging.

"Did anyone ever die of violence in this house?" I asked.

"I've heard rumors, something having to do with the cable car, but I don't know for sure."

We all walked over to the cable car, covered with rust and dirt and long out of commission. Jill placed her hands on it to see if she could get any psychometric impression from it. "This cable car has been much loved, I should say, and much enjoyed." Then her facial expression changed to one of absolute horror. Quickly she took her hands off the cable car.

"What is it, Jill?" I asked.

"Someone came down violently, down the hill in the cable car. Later he wound up here near the pulley."

We walked down to the bottom of the ravine, where there was a magnificent swimming pool. The pool itself was still in operating condition, and there was a pool house on the other side of it. Down here the sound of the music was largely muted, and one could hear one's own voice again. Jill obviously had strong impressions now, and I asked her what she felt about the place.

"I feel that a very vicious man lived here once, but I

don't think he is connected with the name Grace I got before. This may have been at a different time. Oh, he had some dogs, kind of like mastiffs. I think there were two and possibly three. They were vicious dogs, trained to be vicious."

"What did this man do?"

"I see him as a sportsman, quick with words. There were also two young people connected with this man, a boy and a girl. I see them laughing and romping about and having a wonderful time here as teenagers. He seems not to like it at all but is tolerating it. But the dogs seemed to have played a very big part in his life. Nobody would dare enter his property without his permission because of those dogs. Permission, I feel, was rarely given except with a purpose in mind. He has exerted the strongest influence on this house, but I don't think he was the first owner."

"Do you feel that anyone well known was connected with this house?"

"Yes. More than one well-known person, in fact." I asked Jill to describe the personality that she felt was strongest in the atmosphere of the house.

"I see this man with a small moustache, dark thinning hair, exceedingly vain, with a hawklike nose. He has brownish eyes; they have dark circles under them. He doesn't look dissipated by an excess of drink or food, but he does look dissipated through his own excesses. That is, his own mind's excesses. He prides himself on having the eye of the eagle and so affects an eagle-eyed look. I also suspect that he is nearsighted. I see him wearing a lot of smoking jackets. One in particular of maroon color."

The description sounded more and more fascinating. What profession did she think the man followed?

"I see him with a microphone in his hand, also a cigarette and a glass. He might be an actor or he might be a director."

I asked Jill whether this man owned the house or was merely a visitor.

The question seemed to puzzle her. "He might be a visitor, but I see him down here so much he might be staying here. The young people I described before might belong to the owner of the house."

I wondered if the man in the maroon jacket was one of the disturbing entities in the house.

Jill nodded. "I think this man is as well aware now of what he does as when he was alive. *I think he is still here.*"

"Can you get an indication of his name?"

"I get the letter *S*, but that's because he reminds me so much of Salvador Dalí."

"Anything else?"

"Yes, there is an *L* connected with him. The *L* stands for a name like Lay or Lee or Leigh, something like that. Oh, and there is something else. A Royal typewriter is important. I don't know if it's important to him because he writes letters or what, but *Royal* is important."

I was about to turn to the owner of the house when Jill's arm shot up, pointing to the balcony. "That woman up there—she acts very much the owner of the house. I imagine it's Grace." Since none of us could see the woman, I asked Jill for description of what she saw.

"She's a woman in her sixties, with gray or white hair. And it's very neat. She is very statuesque—slender and tall —and she wears a long flowing dress that has pleats all over. She seems to be raising her hand always, very dramatically, like an actress."

I thanked Jill for her work and turned to Marie, the owner of the house. How did all this information stack up with the knowledge she had of the background of her house—for instance, the business of telephones ringing incessantly when there were no telephones about?

"At one time this house was owned by a group of gamblers. They had a whole bunch of telephones all over the house. This goes back several years."

"What about this Grace?"

"The name rings a bell with me, but I can't place it."

"And the baby Heidi keeps hearing?"

"Well, of course, the house used to belong to actor Lionel Barrymore. He and his wife had two babies who died in a fire, although it was not in this house."

Apparently Lionel Barrymore had owned this house, while his brother John lived not far away on Tower Road. Thus John was in a very good position to visit the house frequently. Jill had spoken of a man she saw clairvoyantly as reminding her of Salvador Dalí. That, we all agreed, was a pretty good description of the late John Barrymore. Jill had also mentioned the name Lee or Leigh or something like it. Perhaps she was reaching for Lionel.

The mention of the word *Royal* I found particularly fascinating. On the one hand, the Barrymores were often referred to as the royal family of the theater. On the other hand, if a typewriter was meant, one must keep in mind that John Barrymore had been hard at work on his autobiography in his later years, though he had never completed it. Yet the matter of finishing it had been very much on his mind. As for the teenagers Jill felt around the premises, the two children, Diana and John, Jr., had been at the house a great deal when they were teenagers. John Barrymore, however, didn't like children at all; he merely tolerated them.

I asked Marie (who had been here for more than a year

prior to our visit) if she had ever seen or heard anything uncanny.

"No, but I can feel a presence."

The house has twelve rooms altogether, but according to local tradition, the three bottom rooms were added on somewhat later. "Has anything tragic ever occurred in this house, to your knowledge?"

"A man fell down those stairs head first and was killed. But it was an accident."

Obviously the house had been lived in for many years both before and after the Barrymore tenancy. It seems only natural that other emotional events would leave their mark in the atmosphere of the old house. Despite all this, Jill was able to pick up the personalities of both John and Lionel Barrymore and perhaps even of sister Ethel, if she was the lady in the gray robe. We left the house with a firm promise to dig into the Hall of Records for further verification.

Two weeks later I received a letter from Paula Davidson. She was having lunch with a friend of hers, director William Beaudine, Sr., who had been well acquainted with both John and Lionel Barrymore. Paula mentioned her experience at the house with Jill and me and the description given by Jill of the entity she had felt present in the house. When she mentioned the vicious dogs, Mr. Beaudine remarked that he remembered only too well that John had kept some Great Danes. They might very well have been the vicious dogs described by Jill.

Since that time Paula Davidson has moved away from the house on Summit Ridge. Others have moved in, but no further reports have come to me about the goings-on at the house. If the noisy party we witnessed during our visit was any indication of the present mood of the house, it is most unlikely that the Barrymores will put in an appearance. For if there was one thing the royal family of the theatre disliked, it was noisy competition.

Mr. Belvedere's Ghost, or Clifton Webb's Longest Run

When I was in my twenties Clifton Webb was one of the funniest men on the screen. To me, at least, he represented the epitome of Anglo-Saxon coolness and wit. Only later did I learn that Mr. Webb came from the Midwest and that his English accent and manner were strictly stage-induced. Many people remember his capers as Mr. Belvedere, the deadpan babysitter, and his many other roles in which he portrayed the reserved yet at times explosive character that contained so much of Clifton Webb himself. I saw him on the New York stage in one of Noel Coward's plays, and in the flesh he acted exactly as he had on the screen: cool, deadpan, with a biting, satirical sense of humor.

With the success of his Mr. Belvedere and several motion pictures based upon it, Webb moved into a new-found financial security and consequently went casting about for a home corresponding to his status in the movie industry. His eyes fell upon a white stucco building in one

of the quieter parts of Beverly Hills. The house, set back
somewhat from a side street not far from busy Sunset Boulevard, had a vaguely Spanish-style wing paralleling the
street, to which a shorter wing toward the rear of the
house was attached, creating an enclosed courtyard—again
in the Spanish tradition. The house was and still is surrounded by similar buildings, all of them belonging to the
well-to-do of Beverly Hills. It has had a number of distinguished owners. Grace Moore, the singer, spent some of
her happiest years in it. Later, actor Gene Lockhart lived
there, and his daughter June, who is quite psychic, had a
number of uncanny experiences in it at that time. Clifton
Webb himself was on friendly footing with the world of
the unseen. He befriended Kenny Kingsley, the professional psychic, and on more than one occasion confided
that he had seen Grace Moore's spirit in his house. Evidently the restless spirit of the late singer stayed on in the
house throughout its occupation by Clifton Webb and his
mother, Maybelle. For it appears to me that the "dancing
figure of a woman," which the current lady of the house
has reportedly seen, goes back to the Grace Moore period
rather than to the time of Clifton Webb.

Clifton Webb was inordinately happy in this house. At
the height of his motion picture career, surrounded by
friends, he made up for the arid years of his youth when he
had had to struggle for survival. In 1959 his mother
passed away, bringing an end to a close and sometimes
overpowering relationship. Webb had never married, nor
would he have wanted to. His leanings had never been
hidden from the world, and he was quite content to let
matters be as they were. When his mother died, Webb
became more and more of a recluse. In semi-retirement,
he kept to his house most of the time, seeing fewer friends

as the years went on. In mid-October of 1966 he himself died, almost eight years after his mother. During those eight years, he probably continued his relationship with Maybelle, for Clifton Webb was psychic and believed in life after death. Her clothes and belongings remained in a locked room in the house right up to the time of Clifton's death.

During his twenty years of residence in this house, Webb had remodeled it somewhat and added a room that he dubbed the Greek room, which he had furnished and decorated to his particular taste, taking great care that everything should be exactly as he wanted it to be. By mid-January 1967 the house was on the market. Word of the availability of this house came to the attention of a producer at one of the major motion picture studios in Hollywood. He and his writer-wife had been looking for precisely such a house. Within a matter of days they purchased it and prepared to move in. With the need for redecorating and making certain alterations on the house, the C.'s were not able to move in until sometime in May. Two days before their actual move, they were showing the house to a friend. While they were busy in another part of the house, the gentleman found himself alone in the Greek room. He was wearing contact lenses and felt the need to clean his lenses at that point. There is a bathroom, decorated in gray, off the Greek room. He entered the bathroom, put the contact lenses on the shelf, and turned on the water faucet. When he raised his head from the sink the lenses were no longer there. He searched everywhere but couldn't locate them, and they were never found.

The new owners of the house thought nothing of the matter, but shortly afterward another event took place that shook their confidence. On the first night of their stay in the house Mr. C.'s mother happened to be staying in the Greek room. Unfamiliar with the bathroom, she found herself unable to locate either a toothbrush receptacle or a glass. She therefore left her toothbrush on the sink. The next morning when she entered the bathroom she found the wall receptacle open and exposed and her toothbrush firmly placed into it. Since there had been no one in the room during the night but herself, she became frightened and tried to run from the room. To her amazement the door was locked and resisted opening. In a panic, she fled through the window. Later, calmed down, she returned to the room.

The following morning she awoke in bed and found her cigarettes broken in half, tobacco scattered all over the bed, and the package crushed. It then occurred to Mr. and Mrs. C. that the late Clifton Webb had been vehemently against smoking in his final years.

Earlier that night Mr. and Mrs. C. and Mr. C.'s mother had been standing near the pool in the courtyard. All three were looking toward the house through the master bedroom into what was then Mrs. C.'s bathroom. Suddenly they saw a ghostly swaying figure looking somewhat like the proverbial ectoplasmic ghost. They rubbed their eyes and looked again, but the figure had disappeared.

Over the next few weeks several more apparitions were observed by the C.'s. In the courtyard in front of the house they always saw the same tall gray forms, shadowy yet with some substance. There was no doubt in their minds that they were seeing human figures.

Late in July Mrs. C. was coming home one night around midnight. Stepping into the courtyard, she saw a form like an hourglass (this time completely stationary) in the living room to the left of the couch. Finally she got up enough courage to move closer; when she did so, the form remained still until it gradually dissolved.

All during those first few weeks the animals in the house behaved strangely. The C.'s had several cats and dogs, and whenever they would go to certain spots in the house they would screech in terror and bolt from the area. One of the dogs would not go into the Greek room no matter how much he was coaxed. Instead he would howl at it, and his hackles would rise.

Even the master bedroom was not free from phenomena. Frequently the C.'s would awaken in the middle of the night to the sound of curtains rustling and perceive a form of sorts standing in the corner of the room, observing them.

At first the producer and his wife wondered whether their own imagination and their knowledge of the background of the house were creating fantasies in them. Their doubts were dispelled, however, when they gave a dinner party and were showing a number of guests through the house. One friend, a producer who was staying with the C.'s, suddenly stopped dead while walking from the master bedroom into the hallway, which was then being used as Mr. C.'s study. He claimed he felt something cold enveloping him. Since he is a man not given to hallucinations and has no interest in the occult, his statement carried weight with the C.'s. At the time, the producer employed two servants, a Mexican maid and a butler who slept in a cottage to the rear of the house. On several occasions the maid claimed that a cold presence had attacked her and that lights had gone on and off without explanation. It terrified her and she wanted to know what was going on. The producer could only shake his head, saying he wished he knew himself.

The Greek room seemed to be the center of the activities. Women, especially, staying in the Greek room often had personal articles moved. Mr. C.'s sister, a great skeptic, visited them and was put up in that room. On the third night of her stay she awoke toward dawn feeling a warm, enveloping embrace from behind her. She screamed, jumped out of bed, and turned on the lights. There was no one in the room. The bathroom adjoining that room was also the scene of many experiences. The toilet paper unrolled itself on numerous occasions. Even more fantastic, the toilet had several times been used during the night by parties unknown and left unflushed, even though no human being had been in the bathroom.

In September Mrs. C. took on additional duties as a writer and hired a secretary and assistant who worked in the house with her. But it appeared as if "someone" was not too pleased with the arrangements. All during the winter, things kept disappearing from her office or getting moved about. Her engagement calendar would turn up in the Greek room, and certain files that were kept in cabinets in her office would disappear and turn up in other parts of the house, although no one had placed them there. It appeared that someone was creating havoc in her professional life, perhaps to discourage her or perhaps only to play a prank and put the new owners of the house on notice that a previous resident hadn't quite left.

The worst was yet to come. In October there was an occurrence the C.'s will never forget. All that evening the dog had been howling and running about the house wildly as if anticipating something dreadful. Sounds were heard for which there seemed to be no natural explanation. Then, in the middle of the night, Mr. and Mrs. C. were both awakened by the sound of moaning in their bed-

room, and as they looked up they saw a gray figure form-
ing in the corner of the room.

The next morning they realized they had been through
the night on which Clifton Webb had died, exactly one
year to the day. What they had heard was a reenactment of
that terrible moment. From then on the moaning seemed
to abate.

Although neither Mr. nor Mrs. C. were exactly believers
in the occult, they were open-minded enough to realize
that something was terribly wrong in their house. By now
they knew that the previous owner, most likely Clifton
Webb, was dissatisfied with their presence in the house.
They did not understand why, however. True, they had
made certain changes in the house; they had rearranged
the furniture, and they had used the Greek room as a
guest room. They had also made some changes in the garden and courtyard, especially around the rose bushes,
which had been Mr. Webb's favorites. But was that
enough of a reason for Mr. Webb to want them out of the
house?

In January 1968 they were approached by a real estate
agent, out of the blue, on behalf of a couple who had
passed the house once and immediately become interested
in acquiring it. The C.'s had no intention of selling, so
they named a fantastically high price, thinking this would
end the matter. They discovered to their surprise that the
couple wanted to buy the house anyway. The C.'s then
reconsidered and decided to look for another house. But
they discovered that prices for similar houses had risen so
much that they might as well stay where they were, and
after some discussion they decided to turn down the offer.

That very night Mrs. C. was awakened at 3:30 A.M. by a
rustling sound among the curtains in the master bedroom.

She looked toward the disturbance and noticed an ecto-plasmic form moving across the room and back. As she stared at it in disbelief, she heard a voice saying, "Well, well," over and over. It had the sound of a fading echo and gradually disappeared along with the apparition. Several days in a row Mrs. C. saw the same figure and heard the voice exclaim, as if in amusement, "Well, well, well, well." At the same time, she received the telepathic impression that the ghost was not feeling unfriendly toward her anymore and that he wanted her and her husband to know that he didn't mind their staying on in the house.

By now Mrs. C. was convinced that the ghost was none other than Clifton Webb, and she approached F. M., another producer, who had been a close personal friend of the actor's, with a view toward asking some personal questions about him. When she reported the voice's saying, "Well, well, well, well" over and over, Mr. M. remarked that Webb had been in the habit of saying "well, well" frequently, sometimes for no apparent reason. With that Mrs. C. felt that the identity of the ghostly visitor was firmly established.

That night she was awakened again by a feeling that she was not alone. She looked up and saw the silhouette of a man. *This time it was clearly Clifton Webb.* He was standing just outside the bedroom window in the courtyard. As she looked at the apparition, it occurred to her that he seemed taller than he had been in his movie roles. For what seemed to her several minutes, but may have been only a few seconds, she was able to observe the shadowy apparition of the actor looking into the house directly at her. Shortly afterward it dissolved into thin air. The tall appearance of the figure puzzled her somewhat, so she checked into it. To her amazement she discovered that Webb had actually been six feet tall in life.

A few days later she encountered Mr. Webb again. Her attention was drawn by the strange behavior of her cats, which ran into her office from the courtyard. She was in the habit of taking a shortcut from her office to the kitchen by walking diagonally across the courtyard. As she did so this time, she noticed the tall, erect figure of Mr. Webb in the living room. He seemed to be walking slowly across the living room as if in search of something.

It had become clear to Mr. and Mrs. C. that Webb was not altogether satisfied with the way things were, even though he seemed to be somewhat more friendly toward them. So they invited me to the house to investigate the situation with the help of a reputable psychic. I in turn asked Sybil Leek to come along with me.

On a Thursday night in October 1968 a group of us met at the house. Besides Sybil and me there were my wife, Catherine, Sybil's son Julian, and several people who had known Clifton Webb intimately. They had been asked not out of curiosity but to help identify any material of an evidential nature that might come through Sybil in trance. There was the distinguished playwright Garson Kanin; his actress wife, Ruth Gordon; Rupert Allen, a public relations man who had worked for Webb for many years; and two or three others who had known him.

Sybil, of course, knew nothing about the circumstances of the case, nor why she had been brought to this house. During dinner I was careful to steer the conversation away from the occult, and Sybil and I stayed out of the Greek room. But on her way to the house Sybil had already had her first clairvoyant impression. She described a tall, slender, "sexless" individual who had not been born in California. She also mentioned that she felt the initial *V* or something sounding like it connected with a personality in the house.

After we had grouped ourselves around Sybil in the Greek room, I began the proceedings, as is my custom, by asking the medium for clairvoyant impressions. My hope was that Mr. Webb might pay us a visit, or at any rate tell Sybil what it was that he wanted or what had kept him tied to his former home in so forceful and physical a manner.

"Sybil," I said, "do you get any impressions about the room?"

"I don't like this room," Sybil said sternly. "I wouldn't choose to be in it. I have a strange feeling on my right-hand side toward the window. I feel somebody died here very suddenly. Also I've had for some time now the initial *V* and the word *Meadows* on my mind. I would say this is the least likable room in the house. The strange thing is, I don't feel a male or a female presence; I feel something sexless."

"What sort of person is this?"

"I feel an atmosphere of frustration, an inability to do anything."

"Why is this personality frustrated?"

"Bad relationships."

I decided it was time to begin trance. After brief suggestions Sybil went under quickly and completely. I addressed myself now to the unseen presences in the atmosphere. "Whoever might be present in this room, come forward, please, peacefully and as a friend, so that we may speak to you. We have assembled here as friends. We have come to help you find peace and happiness in this house. Use this instrument, the medium; come peacefully and speak to us so that we may be of help to you in whatever may trouble you."

After a moment Sybil started to toss, eyes closed, breathing heavily. "Can't do it, won't do it. No, I won't do it," she mumbled.

I asked that whoever was speaking through her speak somewhat louder since I had difficulty making out the words. A sardonic smile stole across Sybil's face now, very unlike her own expression. "I'm thirsty, I want a drink, get me a drink."

I promised the entity a drink a little later, but first I wanted to know who it was who had come to speak to us. Instead, Sybil sighed, "It's so cold here, chill, chill. I want to sing and sing. Sing, sing, sing, la, la, la, jolly good time."

"What kind of a song do you want to sing?" I asked, going along with the gag.

"Dead men tell no tales."

"Wouldn't you like to talk to us and tell us about yourself?"

"I want to sing."

"What are you doing here?"

"Writing, writing a song."

"Are you a writer?"

"I do a lot of things."

"What else can you do?"

"Anything, anything."

"Come on, tell me about it."

"No."

"How do I know you can do those things?" I said, using the teasing method now. "You haven't even told me your name."

A snort came from Sybil's lips. "Webb of intrigue."

"What did you say? Would you mind repeating it?"

"Webb, Webb, W-E-B-B."

"Is that your name?"

"Webb, Webb, Webb."

"Why are you here?"

"I need friends."

"Well, you've got them."

"Need friends. I'm lonely. I need to sing."

"Are you a singer?"

"I sing music; music is good."

"Why are you in this particular house?"

"I have a right to be here."

"Tell us why. What does it mean to you?"

"Money, friendship."

"Whose friendship?"

"Where is Wade? Wade, to drink with. People drive me mad."

"What is it that troubles you?" I asked, as softly as I could.

"I won't tell anyone. No help from anyone. There is no help."

"Trust me."

"I'll drink another glass."

"I've come all the way from New York to help you."

"New York—I'll go to New York and watch the people, shows, singing."

"Are you alone?"

"Yes. Nobody wants people like me."

"That isn't true, for we wouldn't be here if we didn't have the feeling of friendship toward you. Why do you think we've come here?"

"Curiosity. There is a reason behind everything. Who are you?"

I explained who I was and that I'd come to try and understand him and if possible set him free from his earthly ties. He had difficulty understanding what I was talking about.

"I want to help you."

"Late."

"Please let me help you."

"Webb."

"Yes, I heard the name," I acknowledged.

"It means nothing."

"I believe there was an actor by that name."

Sybil started to sob now. "Acting, acting all my life."

"What about this house: why are you here?"

"I like it."

"What does it mean to you?"

"What does it mean to me? Lots of money here. Friends. Friends who look after me."

"Do I know them?"

"A newspaperman; I hate newspapermen. Nosy bastards. Let's have a drink. Why don't we have some music?"

"What do you do here all day long?"

"I'm here to drink, look around for a friend or two. I'd like to know a few people. Get some work."

"What kind of work?"

"Contracts. Contracts must be somehow fulfilled."

"Contracts with whom?"

"There's a man called Meadows. Harry Meadows."

"Do you have a contract with him?"

"No good."

"What were you supposed to do?"

"Sign away the house."

"What sort of business is he in?"

"Don't know what to tell you."

"Where did you meet him?"

"He came here. Sixty-four."

"I'd like to help you find peace, Mr. Webb," I said seriously.

The entity laughed somewhat bitterly. "Mr. Webb."

"How else would you want me to call you?"

"Mr. Webb—it's finished."

"Perhaps I can help you."

"Who cares, Cathy."

"Who's Cathy?"

"Where am I, I am lost."

I assured the entity that he was not lost but merely speaking through the medium of another person. Webb obviously had no idea that such things as trance mediumship were possible. He was, of course, quite shocked to find himself in the body of Sybil Leek, even temporarily. I calmed him down and again offered to help. What was it that troubled him most?

"I can't do anything now. I am drunk. I want to sing."

Patiently I explained what his true status was. What he was experiencing were memories from his past; the future was quite different.

"I want to say a lot, but nobody listens."

"I am listening."

"I'm in trouble. Money, drink, Helen."

"What about Helen?"

"I'm peculiar."

"That's your own private affair, and nobody's criticizing you for being peculiar. Also you are very talented."

"Yes." One could tell that he liked the idea of being acclaimed even after his death.

"Now tell me about Helen. Is she in one of your wills?"

"She's dead, you idiot. I wouldn't leave anything to a dead woman. She was after my money."

"What was Helen's full name?"

"Helen T. Meadows."

"How old were you on your last birthday?"

"We don't have birthdays here."

"Ah-ha," I said, "but then you know where you are and what you are."

"I do," the entity said, stretching the *oo* sound with an inimitable comic effect. Anyone who has ever heard Clifton Webb speak on screen or stage would have recognized the sound.

"You know then that you're over there. Good. Then at least we don't have to pretend with each other that I don't know and you don't know."

"I'm tired."

"Was there any other person who knew you and Helen?"

"Cathy, Cathy was a little thing that came around."

"Was there a male friend you might remember by name?"

There was distrust in Sybil's voice when the entity answered. "You're a newspaperman."

"I'm not here as a journalist but primarily to help you. Does the name Conrad mean anything to you?" I'd been told by friends of the late Clifton Webb to ask this. I myself had no idea who this Conrad was or is.

"Hmmm," the entity replied, acknowledging the question. "Initial *V, V* for Victory." At the same time, Sybil took hold of a chain she used as a belt and made an unmistakable gesture as if she were about to strangle someone with it.

"Who was Conrad? Are you trying to show me something?"

Unexpectedly Sybil broke into sobbing again. "Damn you, leave me alone."

The sobbing got heavier and heavier. I decided it was time to release the entity. "Go in peace then; go in peace and never be drawn back to this house where you've had such unhappy experiences. Go and join the loved ones awaiting you on the other side of life. Good-bye, Mr. Webb. Go in peace. Leave this instrument now and let her return to her own body without any memory of what has come through her entranced lips."

A few moments later Sybil awoke, startled, rubbing her eyes and trying to figure out where she was for a moment. "I do feel a bit peculiar," Sybil said, slightly shaken. "Maybe I will have a glass of wine."

After everyone had recovered from the tense attention given to Sybil's trance performance, I invited discussion of what had just transpired. Those who had known Clifton Webb in life volunteered the information that at times Sybil's face had looked somewhat like Webb's, at least to the extent that a woman's face can look like a man's. Her voice, too, had reminded them of the actor's voice—especially in the middle of the session when the trance seemed to have been deepest. As for the names mentioned, Rupert Allen explained that the "Cathy" Sybil had named was a secretary whom Webb had employed for only a week. Also, the Helen Meadows mentioned was probably Helen Mathews, a long-time secretary and assistant of the late actor. There had been a great deal of discussion about a will in which the assistant figured. Quite possibly, Webb and Miss Mathews had been at odds toward the end of his life. As for his wanting to sing, Rupert Allen reminded us that long before Clifton Webb had become a famous actor he had been one of the top song-and-dance men on Broadway, had appeared in many musicals and musical revues, and had always loved the musical theater. The mannerisms and some of the phrases, Mr. Allen confirmed, were very much in the style of Clifton Webb, as was his negative reaction to the idea of having a newspaperman present.

There had been no near relatives living at the time of Webb's death. Under the circumstances the estate, including the house, would go to whomever he had chosen in his will. Was there a second will that had never been found? Was it this need to show the world that a second will existed that kept Clifton Webb tied to his former home?

After the memorable séance with Sybil Leek, I inquired of the owners from time to time whether all was quiet. For a while it was. But then reports of Mr. Webb's reappearance reached me. I realized, of course, that the producer's wife herself, being psychic to a great extent, was supplying some of the energies necessary for Webb to manifest himself in this manner. But I was equally sure that she did not do so consciously. If anything, she wanted a quiet house. But the apparition of Webb and perhaps of Grace Moore, if indeed it was she in the garden, managed to convince Mrs. C. of the reality of psychic phenomena. She no longer feared to discuss her experiences in public. At first her friends looked at her askance, but gradually they came to accept the sincerity and objectivity of her testimony. Others who had never previously mentioned any unusual experiences admitted they had felt chills and uncanny feelings in various parts of the house while visiting the place.

Clifton Webb continues to maintain a foothold in the

house, for better or for worse. Perhaps he likes the attention, or perhaps he's merely looking for that other will. At any rate, he no longer seems to delight in surprising the current owners of the house. After all, they know who he is and what he's up to. Mr. Webb always knew the value of a good entrance. In time, I am sure, he will also know how to make his exit.

Marilyn Monroe's *Unfinished Business*

All these years after Marilyn Monroe died mysteriously at the age of thirty-six, she still makes headlines. Norman Mailer has written a book about her; a photographic exhibit of her life and times drew capacity crowds in Los Angeles; and a national magazine printed some of her unpublished poems as reported by Norman Rosten, a writer who knew her well. Magazines often run cover stories on the late screen star, and her name is still a household word synonymous with sex appeal.

This is not the place to discuss the merits or lack of same surrounding the work of Marilyn Monroe. Others have written of her work as an actress and of her tragic life as a human being, and it is common knowledge that toward the end of her life she was miserable and confused. That she may have taken her life through an overdose of sleeping pills is generally accepted and rarely questioned. Legend has it that she took the pills after losing a role in a comeback film. Other rumors attributed her suicide to a lover's rejection of her. Since the lover was a prominent figure, married at the time, the matter was hushed up in order to keep the breath of scandal away from him.

The coroner's verdict was "probable suicide." There was no evidence that her death was due to either murder or accident, and since an overdose of sleeping pills is generally under the control of the one taking them, the logical conclusion was suicide. With that, the matter was closed.

During the last years of her life, when Marilyn lived as Arthur Miller's wife on New York's East Side, she was befriended by the late John Myers, the English dentist turned medium of whom I have written in many of my books. John Myers was both a psychic healer and an amateur painter. His apartment on Sutton Place was only a short walk from Marilyn Monroe's apartment, and they saw each other on several occasions. Myers suggested that he paint her as the modern Mona Lisa; the screen star, flattered, agreed. (The painting later won a prize at a UNICEF exhibition at the United Nations.) During the times over the years when I worked with Myers, he spoke glowingly of Marilyn Monroe. It was almost as if he had taken her under his wing, to protect her from harm to come. On several occasions he had warned her against sleeping pills. The healing he gave her for her state of neurotic anxiety seemed to relax her for a while. After the news of her sudden passing, Myers placed his portrait of the late screen star in his special healing room.

The room is perhaps the quietest part of his apartment, semidark because of drapes covering the windows. It is here that he does his psychic work. It was in this room that Myers produced, under test conditions, psychic photographs of a late aunt of mine of whom he knew nothing, and of others who were recognized by those present. Among those witnessing the demonstration of psychic photography by Myers were a renowned newspaper columnist and a reporter from one of the wire services.

Shortly after Myers had placed his portrait of Marilyn in his special room, strange things began to happen. Although he was in the habit of turning off the light switch whenever he left the room, he found it turned on again, seemingly of its own volition, on several occasions when he knew that no one else had entered the room. On one occasion he found a personal note in his room that he knew he had not written, nor was there any way in which such a note might have entered the locked room. Unfortunately Myers never disclosed the contents of this note, explaining only that it was a private matter.

Shortly after the incidents with the light switch, Marilyn appeared to the medium. She explained that there had been an accident and that she had had no intention of doing away with herself. As Marilyn explained it to Dr. Myers, she was alone in her home when she received word of being dismissed from the picture she was then making. She tried to find sleep but it wouldn't come. Used to the crutch provided by sleeping pills, she took one after another, forlornly staring out the window. As she drifted into a state of semiconsciousness, she was no longer aware of her motions or the number of pills she had taken. Her senses became dulled, and even if she had wanted to stop or ring for help, she was unable to do so. In one of the accounts dealing with the life of John Myers, *He Walks in Two Worlds* by Maurice Barbanell, Myers is quoted as reporting that Marilyn had said to him, "I did not understand that I was poisoning myself, but it was then too late." After this incident, Marilyn reappeared several times to Myers.

In 1969 I published a number of psychic photographs taken by Myers in a work entitled *Psychic Photography: Threshold of a New Science*. One of the most controversial pictures in this book is a psychic photograph on which at least two dozen portraits appeared. Among the celebrities bunched together in this amazing photograph is Marilyn Monroe, dressed in one of her most glamorous gowns and holding a tablet across her body on which are written the words "Mistake—Not Suicide." The tablet appears to be a piece of paper upon which these words have been typed. That, however, does not necessarily brand this photograph a fake. Since Myers has produced similar photographs under my control and in my presence, I have no reason to consider this photograph anything but authentic.

It would seem, then, that Marilyn was still searching for recognition of the truth of her passing several years after the event itself. This is not unusual in cases where people die tragically or violently before their time. It would appear that Marilyn's most compelling need in the afterlife was to explain to the world that she had not taken her own life but had died as the result of a simple accident.

Susan Cabot is a petite, dark-haired young woman who gained early fame in a number of motion pictures and on the stage. Her singing voice reaches to three octaves, and for a while she was considered one of the most promising new stars on the Hollywood horizon. Shortly after the birth of her first child she withdrew from her career in order to devote herself to the care of her little boy, who had a strange affliction seemingly beyond the capabilities of the medical profession. Now Susan Cabot has again reached out for the limelight. She is returning to the screen, stage, and television, because she has found new truths in meditation and in her involvement with the psychic world.

In April 1972 we sat in her comfortable living room discussing both Susan's own experiences with the shadowy world of ESP and her remembrances of Marilyn Monroe. The house is one of the older residences in Beverly Hills, quiet, well-built in the Spanish style so prominent in the area, and pleasantly cluttered with the mementoes of a busy screen star's life—from photographs to framed letters to books and gifts from admirers.

"When did you first meet Marilyn Monroe?"

"I was called to Columbia to do a film. Freddy in the music department introduced us. She came to practice her singing. She loved music, and she was singing 'Those Little White Lies.' We shared some music lessons."

"Did you meet her socially afterward?"

"Yes. When we first met, we went together everywhere, including some parties, because I was terrified of dating. I had just come from New York. There was such a strong bond between us—"

"You mean like telepathy?"

"Yes. She would start a sentence and I'd finish it for her."

"Did you ever discuss psychic phenomena? Was there an interest in that?"

"No, because I had only the most intellectual contact with everybody. The main thing was that we were both born to be serious artists and not just sex symbols, and we didn't want to just date and be thrown about, and so we found safety in dating together."

"What happened when you heard of her death?"

"I didn't believe she had committed suicide."

"Was there any contact between her and you after her death?"

"Yes."

"What sort of thing?"

"It was as if she were saying, 'Do you remember when I said this?' That was the first time. This feeling . . . I can't call it an apparition. I can't say I heard anything. I can't say I saw anything. But I felt the presence of Marilyn at my shoulders. It was as if, when this presence was felt, she reminded me of the last time I saw her. At the time, we hadn't seen each other for a long period. I felt that she didn't remember me any longer. She was surrounded by a lot of people. Now, standing next to me, she was reminding me of this incident. She looked at me for a split second, and suddenly I felt oblivious of who *I* was. She narrowed her eyes and said, 'What am I doing here?' Then she said, 'I didn't mean to do this, you know I didn't mean to do this,' and she began to cry, and I was crying, too."

"She didn't mean to do it? How did it happen then?"

"She was in terrible pain."

"So she took these pills?"

"She couldn't stand it. She took the pills to go to sleep."

"Did she ever indicate to you that she would want somebody to know about this?"

"I don't know. I just know she was pleading for understanding. It wasn't just a message."

"Do you think she is troubled?"

"She's still confused."

"Do you think she is aware of her own death?"

"I see her hunched over, begging." Susan shrugged.

* * *

Susan Cabot is no stranger to psychic phenomena herself. When she lived in New York she had one of the most harrowing experiences with the world beyond the flesh. She was living at the time in one of those little apartments consisting of one room and an alcove for the bed. This particular apartment was on top of a French restaurant and there was an electric sign on the outside of the building. The windows were barred both in the living room and in the alcove above it, because there was a roof extending over the alcove where people might conceivably try to enter the apartments below. That particular night Susan couldn't sleep. She was tossing in bed wondering about her future. Suddenly she became aware of a presence in her room. It looked like a light flashing on and off, coming to her from the ceiling. There was no rational explanation for such a light, so at first she thought it was her vivid imagination. Imagine her horror when she suddenly saw the light turn into a figure of what looked like a musketeer from another age! His grim face with a slightly hooked nose stared at her in the most unfriendly manner. In his hand he had a dagger, which he now raised as if to strike at her. During this time there was no sound whatsoever.

A musketeer in a Fifty-sixth Street apartment in New York City? Was Susan's motion picture imagination perhaps running away with her? I immediately questioned her about the apparition.

"Did he look three-dimensional?"

"Absolutely."

"What did you do?"

"I wanted to scream, but I couldn't. I was frightened, and I pleaded with him silently—'Don't kill me, please don't kill me.' I was looking at him while saying this. I didn't dare move. I was trapped. I knew if I moved, it would be the end of me."

"How did it end?"

"He listened and turned around. He lowered his dagger."

"Did he speak?"

"No. But I didn't feel his hatred as much."

"How did he disappear?"

"Through the wall."

"Walking?"

"I saw his cape vanish into the darkness."

"Did you hear anything?"

"The swish of the cape."

"Did he ever come back?"

"Yes. The next night."

"Did he look the same?"

"No. He was smiling."

"Did he have the dagger?"

"No. But his hand lay on his belt."

"Was he still filled with hatred?"

"No. It was as though he had had his victims. It was like the smile of victory."

"Did he return after that?"

"There were three more times. He was there right by my side. He didn't enter from anywhere—he was just there."

"How did he leave?"

"He disappeared. I didn't hear anything. I didn't even see him go, as I did the first time. Years later he appeared again when I had my baby. I then lived across town in a penthouse."

"What did you see?"

"I was facing west and there was this enormous window and the balcony. I didn't see anything, but I felt him."

"How did you know that it was *him?*"

"I knew. At the same time, I physically saw an Indian trying to get into the room. The Indian tried to get to the baby. But the musketeer came as if to help me."

"Was this the last time you have seen or felt him?"

"Once or twice I felt a presence, but I'm not sure it was him."

"But who is he? Is he trying to protect you? What is the reason for his contact?"

"I don't know."

Recently Susan has been able to help various friends through her ESP ability. She gets flashes about future events and passes them on freely, in the hope that she can help people avert problems or tragedy. She doesn't consider herself a professional psychic by any means but wants to develop her innate talent in this respect. To her it is all a great surprise. Somehow she feels she has lived before, and that some of the people who have come to her in this life have shared experiences with her in another existence. She wants very much to know who she was, because it will help her understand better who she is now. Susan, with all her beauty and talents, has much in common with the late Marilyn Monroe. She too is forever searching for her sense of identity and mission.

The Ill-Fated Kennedys

"When are you going to go down to Dallas and find out about President Kennedy?" the pleasant visitor inquired. He was a schoolteacher who had come to me to seek advice on how to start a course in parapsychology in his part of the country.

The question about President Kennedy was hardly new. I had been asked the same question in various forms ever since the assassination of John F. Kennedy, as if I and my psychic helpers had the duty to use our combined talents to find out what really happened at the School Book Depository in Dallas. I suppose similar conditions prevailed after the death of Abraham Lincoln. People's curiosity had been aroused, and with so many unconfirmed rumors making the rounds the matter of a president's sudden death does become a major topic of conversation and inquiry.

I wasn't there when Lincoln was shot, but I was around when President Kennedy was murdered. Thus I am in a fairly good position to trace the public interest with the assassination from the very start.

I assured my visitor that so far I had no plans to go down to Dallas with a medium to find out what "really" happened. I have said so on television many times. When I was reminded that the Abraham Lincoln murder also left some unanswered questions and that I had indeed investigated it and come up with startlingly new results in my book *Window to the Past,* I responded that there was one basic difference between the Kennedy death and the assassination of President Lincoln: Lincoln's ghost has been seen repeatedly by reliable witnesses in the White House; so far I have not received any reliable reports of ghostly sightings concerning the late President Kennedy. In my opinion, this meant that the restlessness that caused Lincoln to remain in what used to be his working world has not caused John F. Kennedy to do likewise.

But I am not a hundred percent sure any longer. Having learned how difficult it is to get information about such matters in Washington, or to gain admission to the White House as anything but a casual tourist—or, of course, on official business—I am also convinced that much may be suppressed or simply disregarded by those to whom experiences have happened simply because we live in a time when psychic phenomena can still embarrass those to whom they occur, especially if they are in a position of importance.

But even if John Fitzgerald Kennedy is not walking the corridors of the White House at night, bemoaning his untimely demise or trying to right the many wrongs that have happened in this country since he left us, he is apparently doing something far better. He communicates, under special conditions and with special people. He is far from "dead and gone," if I am to believe those to whom these experiences have come. Naturally, one must sift the fantasy from the real thing—even more so when we are dealing with a famous person. I have done so, and I have looked very closely at the record of people who have reported to me psychic experiences dealing with the Kennedy family. I have eliminated a number of such reports because I had doubts about the emotional stability of those who had made the reports. I have also eliminated many other reports that were far too general and vague to be evidential even in the broadest sense. Material that was unsupported by witnesses, or material that was presented after the fact, was of course disregarded.

With all that in mind, I have come to the conclusion that the Kennedy destiny was something that could not have been avoided whether or not one accepts the old Irish Kennedy curse as factual.

Even the ghostly Kennedys are part and parcel of American life at the present. Why they must pay so high a price in suffering, I cannot guess. But it is true that the Irish forebears of the American Kennedys have also suffered an unusually high percentage of violent deaths over the years, mainly on the male side of the family. There is a tradition that way back in the Middle Ages a Kennedy was cursed for having incurred the wrath of some private local enemy. As a result of the curse, he and all his male descendants were to die violently one by one. To dismiss curses as fantasies, or at the very best workable only because of fear symptoms, would not be accurate. I had great doubts about the effectiveness of curses until I came across several cases that allowed for no other explanation. In particular, I refer back to the case of the Wurmbrand curse reported by me in *Ghosts of the Golden West*. In that case the last male descendant of an illustrious family died under mysterious circumstances quite unexpectedly even while under the care of doctors in a hospital. Thus, if the Kennedy curse is operative, nothing much can be done about it.

Perhaps I should briefly explain the distinction between ghosts and spirits here, since so much of the Kennedy material is of the latter kind rather than the former. Ghosts are generally tied to houses or definite places where their physical bodies died tragically, or at least in a state of unhappiness. They are unable to leave the premises, so to speak, and can only repeat the pattern of their final moments, and are for all practical purposes not fully cognizant of their true state. They can be compared with psychotics in the physical state, and must first be freed from their own self-imposed delusions to be able to answer, if possible through a trance medium, or to leave and become free spirits out in what Dr. Joseph Rhine of Duke University has called "the world of the mind," which I generally refer to as the nonphysical world.

Spirits, on the other hand, are people who have left the physical body but are very much alive in a thinner, etheric body, with which they are able to function pretty much the same as they did in the physical body, except that they are now no longer weighted down by physical objects, distances, time, and space. The majority of those who die become free spirits, though a tiny fraction are unable to proceed into the next stage and must remain behind because of emotional difficulties. Those who have gone on are not necessarily gone forever; to the contrary they are able and frequently anxious to keep a hand in situations they have left unfinished on the earth plane. Death by violence or under tragic conditions does not necessarily create a ghost. Some such conditions may indeed create the ghost syndrome, but many others do not. It seems that President Kennedy is in the latter group—that is to say, a free spirit capable of continuing an interest in the world he left behind, as I will show in the next pages.

The R. Lumber Company is a prosperous firm specializing in the manufacture and wholesale of lumber. It is located in Georgia and the owners, Mr. and Mrs. Bernard R., are respected citizens in their community. Mrs. R. contacted me in April 1970. "I have just finished reading your book *Life After Death,* and could not resist your invitation to share a strange experience with you," she explained, "hoping that you can give me some opinion regarding its authenticity.

"I have not had an opportunity to discuss what happened with anyone who is in any way psychic or clairvoyant. I have never tried to contact anyone close to the Kennedys about this, as of course I know they must have received thousands of letters. Many times I feel a little guilty about not even trying to contact Mrs. Kennedy and the children, if indeed it could have been a genuine last message from the president. It strikes me as odd that we might have received it or imagined we received it. We were never fans of the Kennedys, and although we were certainly sympathetic to the loss of our president, we were not as emotionally upset as many of our friends who were ardent admirers.

"I am in no way psychic, nor have I ever had any supernatural experience before. I am a young homemaker and businesswoman, and cannot offer any possible explanation for what happened.

"On Sunday night, November 24, 1963, following John F. Kennedy's assassination, my family and I were at home watching on television the procession going through the Capital paying their last respects. I was feeling very depressed, especially since that afternoon Lee Oswald had also been killed and I felt we would never know the full story of the assassination. For some strange reason, I suddenly thought of the Ouija board, although I have never taken the answers seriously and certainly have never before consulted it about anything of importance. I asked my teenage daughter to work the board with me, and we went into another room. I had never tried to 'communicate with the dead.' I don't know why I had the courage to ask the questions I did on that night, but somehow, I felt compelled to go on.

Question: Will our country be in danger without Kennedy?

Answer: Strong with, weak without Kennedy, plot—stop.

Question: Will Ruby tell why president was killed?

Answer: Ruby does not know, only Oswald and I know. Sorry.

Question: Will we ever know why Kennedy was killed?

Answer: Underground and Oswald know, Ruby does not know, gangland leader caught in plot.

Question: Who is gangland leader?

Answer: Can't tell now.

Question: Why did Oswald hate president?

Answer: Negroes, civil rights bill.

Question: Have Oswald's and Kennedy's spirits met?

Answer: Yes. No hard feelings in Heaven.

Question: Are you in contact with Kennedy?

Answer: Yes.

Question: Does Kennedy have a message he would send through us?

Answer: Yes, yes, yes, tell J., C., and J.J. about this. Thanks, JFK.

Question: Can Kennedy give us some nickname to authenticate this?

Answer: Only nickname 'John John.'

Question: Do you really want us to contact someone?

Answer: Yes, but wait 'til after my funeral.

Question: How can we be sure Jackie will see our letter?

Answer: Write personal, not sympathy business.

Question: Is there something personal you could tell us to confirm this message?

Answer: Prying public knows all.

Question: Just one nickname you could give us?

Answer: J.J. (John John) likes to swim lots, called 'Daddy's little swimmer boy.' Does that help? JFK.

Question: Anything else?

Answer: J.J. likes to play secret game and bunny.

Question: What was your Navy Serial number?

Answer: 109 P.T. (jg) Skipper–5905. [*Seemed confused.*]

Question: Can we contact you again?

Answer: You, JFK, not JFK you.

Question: Give us address of your new home.

Answer: Snake Mountain Road.

Question: Will Mrs. Kennedy believe this, does she believe in the supernatural?

Answer: Some—tired—that's all tonight.

"At this point the planchette slid off the bottom of the board marked 'Good-by' and we attempted no further questions that night.

"The board at all times answered our questions swiftly and deliberately, without hesitation. It moved so rapidly, in fact, that my daughter and I *could not keep up with the message as it came.* We called out the letters to my eleven-year-old daughter, who wrote them down, and we had to unscramble the words *after* we had received the entire message. We *had no intention* of trying to communicate *directly* with President Kennedy. I cannot tell you how frightened I was when I asked if there was a message he would send and the message came signed 'JFK.'

"For several days after, I could not believe the message was genuine. I have written Mrs. Kennedy several letters trying to explain what happened, but have never had the courage to mail them.

"None of the answers obtained are sensational, most are things we could have known or guessed. The answers given about 'John John' and 'secret game' and 'bunny' were in a magazine which my children had read and I had not. However, the answer about John John being called 'Daddy's little swimmer boy' is something none of us have ever heard or read. I have researched numerous articles written about the Kennedys during the last two years and have not found any reference to this. I could not persuade my daughter to touch the board again for days. We tried several times in December 1963, but were unsuccessful. One night, just before Christmas, a friend of mine persuaded my daughter to work the board with her. Perhaps the most surprising message came at this time, and it was also the last one we ever received. We are all Protestant and the message was inconsistent with our religious beliefs. When they asked if there was a message from President Kennedy, the planchette spelled out immediately, 'Thanks for your prayers while I was in Purgatory, JFK.' "

I have said many times in print and on television that I take a dim view of Ouija boards in general. Most of the material obtained from the use of this instrument merely reflects the unconscious of one or both sitters. Occasionally, however, Ouija boards have been able to tap the psychic levels of a person and come up with the same kind of veridical material a clairvoyant might come up with. Thus, to dismiss the experiences of Mrs. R. merely because the material was obtained through a Ouija board would not be fair. Taking into account the circumstances, the background of the operators, and their seeming reluctance to seek out such channels of communication, I must dismiss ulterior motives such as publicity-seeking reasons or idle curiosity as being the causative factor in the event. On the other hand, having just watched a television program dealing with the demise of President Kennedy, the power of suggestion might have come into play. Had the material obtained through the Ouija board been more specific to a greater extent, perhaps I would not hesitate to label this a genuine experience. While there is nothing in the report that indicates fraud—either conscious or unconscious— there is nothing startling in the information given. Surely, if the message had come from Kennedy, or if Kennedy himself had been on the other end of the psychic line, there would have been certain pieces of information that would have been known only to him and that could yet be checked out in a way that was accessible. Surely, Kennedy would have realized how difficult it might have been for an ordinary homemaker to contact his wife. Thus, it seems to me that some other form of proof of identity would have been furnished. This, however, is really only speculation. Despite the sincerity of those reporting the incident, I feel that there is reasonable doubt as to the genuineness of the communication.

* * *

By far the majority of communications regarding President Kennedy relate to his death and are in the nature of premonitions, dreams, visions, and other warnings prior to or simultaneous with the event itself. The number of such experiences indicates that the event itself must have been felt ahead of its realization, indicating that some sort of law was in operation that could not be altered, even if President Kennedy could have been warned. As a matter of fact, I am sure that he was given a number of warnings, and that he chose to disregard them. I don't see how he could have done otherwise—both because he was the president and out of a fine sense of destiny that is part and parcel of the Kennedy make-up. Certainly Jeane Dixon was in a position to warn the president several times prior to the assassination. Others, less well connected in Washington, might have written letters that had never gotten through to the president. Certainly one cannot explain these things away merely by saying that a public figure is always in danger of assassination, or that Kennedy had incurred the wrath of many people in this country and abroad. This simply doesn't conform to the facts. Premonitions have frequently been very precise, indicating in more or less great detail the manner, time, and nature of the assassination. If it were merely a matter of vaguely foretelling the sudden death of the president, then of course one could say that this comes from a study of the situation or from a general feeling about the times in which we live. But this is not so. Many of the startling predictions couldn't have been made by anyone, unless they themselves were in on the planning of the assassination.

* * *

Mrs. Rose LaPorta lives in suburban Cleveland, Ohio. Over the years she has developed her ESP faculties—partially in the dream state and partially while awake. Some of her premonitory experiences are so detailed that they cannot be explained on the basis of coincidence, if there is such a thing, or in any other rational terms. For instance, on May 10, 1963, she dreamed she had eaten something with glass in it. She could even feel it in her mouth, so vividly that she began to spit it out and woke up. On October 4 of the same year, after she had forgotten the peculiar dream, she happened to be eating a cookie. There was some glass in it, and her dream became reality in every detail. Fortunately, she had told several witnesses of her original dream, so she was able to prove this to herself on the record.

At her place of work there is a superintendent named Smith, who has offices in another city. There never was any close contact with that man, so it was rather startling to Mrs. LaPorta to hear a voice in her sleep telling her, "Mr. Smith died at home on Monday." Shocked by this message, she discussed it with her coworkers. That was on May 18, 1968. On October 8 of the same year, an announcement was made at the company to the effect that "Mr. Smith died at home on Monday, October 7."

Mrs. LaPorta's ability to tune in on future events reached a national subject on November 17, 1963. She dreamed she was at the White House in Washington on a dark, rainy day. There were beds set up in each of the porticoes. She found herself, in the dream, moving from one bed to another, because she wanted to shelter herself from the rain. There was much confusion going on and many men were running around in all directions. They seemed to have guns in their hands and pockets. Finally,

Mrs. LaPorta, in the dream, asked someone what was happening, and they told her they were Secret Service men. She was impressed with the terrible confusion and atmosphere of tragedy when she awoke from her dream. That was five days before the assassination happened on November 22, 1963. The dream is somewhat reminiscent of the famed Abraham Lincoln dream, in which he himself saw his own body on the catafalque in the East Room, and asked who was dead in the White House. I have reported on that dream in *Window to the Past.*

Marie Howe is a Maryland housewife, fifty-two years old, and only slightly psychic. The night before the assassination she had a dream in which she saw two brides with the features of men. Upon awakening she spoke of her dream to her husband and children, and interpreted it that someone was going to die very soon. She thought that two persons would die close together. The next day, Kennedy and Oswald turned into the "brides of death" she had seen in her dream.

Bertha Zelkin lives in Los Angeles. The morning of the assassination she suddenly found herself saying, "What would we do if President Kennedy were to die?" That afternoon the event took place.

Marion Confalonieri is a forty-one-year-old housewife, a native of Chicago, has worked as a secretary, and lives with her husband, a draftsman, and two daughters in a comfortable home in California. Over the years she has had many psychic experiences, ranging from déjà vu feelings to psychic dreams. On Friday, November 22, the assassination took place and Oswald was captured the same day.

The following night, Saturday, November 23, Mrs. Confalonieri went to bed exhausted and in tears from all the commotion. Some time during the night she dreamed that she saw a group of men, perhaps a dozen, dressed in suits and some with hats. She seemed to be floating a little above them, looking down on the scene, and she noticed that they were standing very close in a group. Then she heard a voice say, "Ruby did it." The next morning she gave the dream no particular thought. The name Ruby meant absolutely nothing to her, nor, for that matter, to anyone else in the country at that point. It wasn't until she turned her radio on and heard the announcement that Oswald had been shot by a man named Ruby that she realized she had had a preview of things to come several hours before the event itself had taken place.

Another one who tuned in on the future a little ahead of reality was the famed British author Pendragon, whose real name was L. T. Ackerman. In October 1963, he wrote, "I wouldn't rule out the possibility of attempted assassination or worse if caught off guard." He wrote to President Kennedy urging him that his guard be strengthened, especially when appearing in public.

Dr. Robert G. is a dentist who makes his home in Rhode Island. He has had psychic experiences all his life, some of which I have described elsewhere. At the time when Oswald was caught by the authorities, the doctor's wife wondered out loud what would happen to the man. Without thinking about what he was saying, Dr. G. replied, "He will be shot in the police station." The words just popped out of his mouth. There was nothing to indicate even a remote possibility of such a course of action.

He also had a premonition that Robert Kennedy would
be shot, but he thought that the senator would live on
with impaired faculties. We know, of course, that Senator
Kennedy died. Nevertheless, as most of us will remember,
for a time after the announcement of the shooting there
was hope that the senator would indeed continue to live,
although with impaired faculties. Not only did the doctors
think that might be possible, but announcements were
made to that effect. Thus, it is entirely feasible that Dr. G.
tuned in not only on the event itself but also on the
thoughts and developments that were part of the event.

As yet we know very little about the mechanics of
premonitions, and it is entirely possible that some psychics
cannot fine-tune their inner instruments beyond a general
pickup of future material. This seems to relate to the inability of most mediums to pinpoint exact time in their
predictions.

Cecilia Fawn Nichols is a writer who lives in Twenty-
nine Palms, California. All her life she has had premonitions that have come true and has accepted the psychic in
her life as a perfectly natural element. She had been root-
ing for John F. Kennedy to be elected president because
she felt that his Catholicism made him a kind of underdog.
When he finally did get the nod, Miss Nichols found herself far from jubilant. As if something foreboding were
preying heavily on her mind, she received the news of his
election glumly and with a feeling of disaster. At the time
she could not explain to herself why, but the thought that
the young man who had just been elected was condemned
to death entered her mind. "When the unexpected passes
through my mind, I know I can expect it," she explained.
"I generally do not know just how or when or what. In

this case I felt some idiot was going to kill him because of his religion. I expected the assassination much sooner. Possibly because of domestic problems, I wasn't expecting it when it did happen."

On Sunday morning, November 24, she was starting breakfast. Her television set was tuned to Channel 2, and she decided to switch to Channel 7 because that station had been broadcasting the scene directly from Dallas. The announcer was saying that any moment now Oswald would be brought out of jail to be taken away from Dallas. The camera showed the grim faces of the crowd. Miss Nichols took one look at the scene and turned to her mother. "Mama, come in the living room. Oswald is going to be killed in a few minutes, and I don't want to miss seeing it."

There was nothing to indicate such a course of action, of course, but the words just came out of her mouth as if motivated by some outside force. A moment later, the feared event materialized. Along with the gunshot, however, she distinctly heard words said that she was never again to hear on any rerun of the televised action. The words were spoken just as Ruby lifted his arm to shoot. As he began pressing the trigger, the words and the gunshot came close together. Afterward Miss Nichols listened carefully to many of the reruns but never managed to hear the words again. None of the commentators mentioned them. No account of the killing mentions them. And yet Miss Nichols clearly heard Ruby make a statement even as he was shooting Oswald down.

The fact that she alone heard the words spoken by Ruby bothered Miss Nichols. In 1968 she was with a group of friends discussing the Oswald killing, and again she reported what she had heard that time on television. There was a woman in that group who nodded her head. She too had heard the same words. It came as a great relief to Miss Nichols to know that she was not alone in her perception. The words Ruby spoke as he was shooting Oswald were words of anger: "Take this, you son of a bitch!"

This kind of psychic experience is far closer to truthful tuning in on events as they transpire, or just as they are formulating themselves, than some of the more complicated interpretations of events after they have happened.

Two Cincinnati amateur mediums by the names of Dorothy Barrett and Virginia Hill, who have given out predictions of things to come to the newspapers from time to time, also made some announcements concerning the Kennedy assassination. I have met the two ladies at the home of the Straders in Cincinnati, at which time they seemed to be imitating the Edgar Cayce readings in that they pinpointed certain areas of the body subject to illness. Again, I met Virginia Hill recently and was confronted with what she believes is the personality of Edgar Cayce, the famous seer of Virginia Beach. Speaking through her, I questioned the alleged Edgar Cayce entity and took notes, which I then asked Cayce's son, Hugh Lynn Cayce, to examine for veridity. Regrettably, most of the answers proved to be incorrect, thus making the identity of Edgar Cayce highly improbable. Nevertheless, Virginia Hill is psychic and some of her predictions have come true.

On December 4, 1967, the Cincinnati *Inquirer* published many of her predictions for the following year. One of the more startling statements is that there were sixteen people involved in the Kennedy assassination, according to Virginia's spirit guide, and that the leader was a woman.

Oswald, it is claimed, did not kill the president, but a policeman (now dead) did.

In this connection it is interesting to note that Sherman Skolnick, a researcher, filed suit in April 1970 against the National Archives and Records Services to release certain documents concerning the Kennedy assassination—in particular, Skolnick claimed that there had been a prior Chicago assassination plot in which Oswald and an accomplice by the name of Thomas Arthur Vallee and three or four other men had been involved. Their plan to kill the president at a ball game had to be abandoned when Vallee was picked up on a minor traffic violation the day before the game. Skolnick, according to *Time* magazine of April 20, 1970, firmly believes that Oswald and Vallee and several others were linked together in the assassination plot.

When it comes to the assassination of Senator Robert Kennedy, the picture is somewhat different. To begin with, very few people thought that Robert Kennedy was in mortal danger, while John F. Kennedy, as president, was always exposed to political danger—as are all presidents. The senator was not in quite so powerful a position. True, he had his enemies, as have all politicians. But the murder by Sirhan Sirhan came as much more of a surprise than the assassination of his brother. It is thus surprising that so much premonitory material exists concerning Robert Kennedy as well. In a way, of course, this material is even more evidential because of the lesser likelihood of such an event transpiring.

Mrs. Elaine Jones lives in San Francisco. Her husband is a retired businessman; her brother-in-law headed the publishing firm of Harper & Row; and she is not given to hallucinations. I have reported some of her psychic experiences elsewhere. Shortly before the assassination of Robert Kennedy she had a vision of the White House front. At first she saw it as it was and is, and then suddenly the entire front seemed to crumble before her eyes. To her this meant death of someone connected with the White House. A short time later, the assassination of the senator took place.

Months before the event, famed Washington seeress Jeane Dixon was speaking at the Hotel Ambassador in Los Angeles. She said that Robert Kennedy would be the victim of a "tragedy right here in this hotel." The Senator was assassinated there eight months later.

A young Californian by the name of Lorraine Caswell had a dream the night before the assassination of Senator Kennedy. In her dream she saw the actual assassination as it later happened. The next morning, she reported her nightmare to her roommate, who had served as witness on previous occasions of psychic premonition.

Ellen Roberts works as a secretary, telephonist, and part-time volunteer for political causes. During the campaign of Senator Robert Kennedy she spent some time at headquarters volunteering her services. Miss Roberts is a member of the Reverend Zenor's Hollywood Spiritualist Temple. Reverend Zenor, while in trance, speaks with the voice of Agasha, a higher teacher, who is also able to foretell events in the future. On one such occasion, long before the assassination of John F. Kennedy, Agasha— through Reverend Zenor—had said, "There will be not one assassination, but two. He will also be quite young.

Victory will be almost within his grasp, but he will die just before he assumes the office, if it cannot be prevented."

The night of the murder, Ellen Roberts fell asleep early. She awakened with a scene of Robert Kennedy and President Kennedy talking. John F. Kennedy was putting his arm around his brother's shoulders and she heard him say, "Well, Bobby, you made it—the hard way." With a rueful smile they walked away. Miss Roberts took this to mean the discomfort that candidate Robert Kennedy had endured during the campaign—the rock-throwing, the insults, the name-callings. Never once did she accept it as anything more sinister. The following day she realized what her vision had meant.

A curious thing happened to Mrs. Lewis H. MacKibbel. She and her ten-year-old granddaughter were watching television the evening of June 4, 1968. Suddenly the little girl jumped up, clasped her hands to her chest, and in a shocked state announced, "Robert Kennedy has been shot. Shot down, Mama." Her sisters and mother teased her about it, saying that such an event would have been mentioned on the news if it were true. After a while the subject was dropped. The following morning, June 5, when the family radio was turned on, word of the shooting came. Startled, the family turned to the little girl, who could only nod and say, "Yes I know. I knew it last night."

Mrs. Dawn Chorley lives in central Ohio. A native of England, she spent many years with her husband in South Africa, and has had psychic experiences at various times in her life. During the 1968 election campaign she and her husband, Colin Chorley, had been working for Eugene

McCarthy, but when Robert Kennedy won the primary in New Hampshire she was very pleased with that too. The night of the election, she stayed up late. She was very keyed up and thought she would not be able to sleep because of the excitement, but contrary to her expectations she fell immediately into a very deep sleep around midnight. That night she had a curious dream.

"I was standing in the central downstairs room of my house. I was aware of a strange atmosphere around me and felt very lonely. Suddenly I felt a pain in the left side of my head, toward the back. The inside of my mouth started to crumble and blood started gushing out of my mouth. I tried to get to the telephone, but my arms and legs would not respond to my will; everything was disoriented. Somehow I managed to get to the telephone and pick up the receiver. With tremendous difficulty I dialed for the operator, and I could hear a voice asking whether I needed help. I tried to say, 'Get a doctor,' but the words came out horribly slurred. Then came the realization I was dying and I said, 'Oh my God, I am dying,' and sank into oblivion. I was shouting so loud I awoke my husband, who is a heavy sleeper. Shaking off the dream, I still felt terribly depressed. My husband, Colin, noticed the time. Allowing for time changes, it was the exact minute Robert Kennedy was shot."

Jill Taggart of North Hollywood, California, has been working with me as a developing medium for several years now. By profession a writer and model, she has been her own worst critic, and in her report avoids anything that cannot be substantiated. On May 14, 1968, she had meant to go to a rally in honor of Senator Robert Kennedy in Van Nuys, California. Since the parade was only three blocks from her house, it was an easy thing for her to walk over. But early in the evening she had resolved not to go. To begin with, she was not fond of the senator, and she hated large crowds, but more than anything she had a bad feeling that something would happen to the senator while he was in his car. On the news that evening she heard that the senator had been struck in the temple by a flying object and had fallen to his knees in the car. The news also reported that he was all right. Jill, however, felt that the injury was more serious than announced and that the senator's reasoning faculties would be impaired henceforth. "It's possible that it could threaten his life," she reported. "I know that temples are tricky things." When I spoke to her further, pressing for details, she indicated that she had then felt disaster for Robert Kennedy, but her logical mind refused to enlarge upon the comparatively small injury the candidate had suffered. A short time later, of course, the Senator was dead—not from a stone thrown at him but from a murderer's bullet. Jill Taggart had somehow tuned in on both events simultaneously.

Seventeen-year-old Debbie Gaurlay, a high school student who also works training horses, has had ESP experiences for several years. Two days prior to the assassination of Robert Kennedy she remarked to a friend by the name of Debbie Corso that the senator would be shot very shortly. At that time there was no logical reason to assume an attempt upon the senator's life.

John Londren is a machine fitter, twenty-eight years old, who lives with his family in Hartford, Connecticut. Frequently he has had dreams of events that have later transpired. In March 1968 he had a vivid dream in which

he saw Senator Robert Kennedy shot while giving his In-
augural Address. Immediately he told his wife and father
about the dream, and even wrote a letter to the senator in
April but decided not to send it until after the election.
Even the correct names of the assassin and of two people
present occurred in his dream. But Mr. Londren dismissed
the dream since he knew that Roosevelt Grier and Rafe
Johnson were sports figures. He felt they would be out of
place in a drama involving the assassination of a political
candidate. Nevertheless, those were the two men who actually subdued the killer.

In a subsequent dream he saw St. Patrick's Cathedral in
New York during Senator Kennedy's funeral. People were
running about in a state of panic, and he had the feeling
that a bombing or shooting had taken place. So upset was
Mr. Londren by his second dream that he asked his father,
who had a friend in Washington, to make some inquiries.
Eventually the information was given to a Secret Service
man who respected extrasensory perception. The New
York City bomb squad was called in and the security
around the Cathedral was doubled. A man with an un-
loaded gun was caught fifteen minutes before the president arrived for the funeral at the Cathedral. Mr. Londren's second dream thus proved to be not only evidential
but of value in preventing what might have been another
crime.

Another amateur prophet is Elaine Morganelli, a Los
Angeles housewife. In May 1967 she predicted in writing
that President Johnson would be assassinated on June 4,
and sent this prediction along with others to her brother,
Lewis Olson. What she actually had heard was "President
assassination June 4." Well, President Johnson was not as-

sassinated, but on June 5, 1968, Robert Kennedy, a presidential candidate, was shot to death.

A sixteen-year-old teenager from Tennessee named John Humphreys experienced a vision late in 1963, while he was in bed but not yet fully asleep. As he looked at the floor of his room he saw several disembodied heads. One of the heads was that of President Kennedy, who had just been assassinated. The others, he did not recognize at the time. Later, he realized who they had been. One was the head of Robert Kennedy; the other of Martin Luther King. He had the feeling at the time of the vision that all three men would be shot in the head. (He also remembered two other heads—that of a Frenchman and of a very large Englishman—but no names.)

On April 16, 1968, a Canadian by the name of Mrs. Joan Holt wrote to the *Evening Standard* premonition bureau, conducted by science editor Peter Fairley, "Robert Kennedy to follow in his brother's footsteps and face similar danger."

"There is going to be a tragic passing in the Kennedy family very soon," said British medium Minie Bridges at a public sitting the last week of May 1968.

It seems clear to me that even the death of Senator Kennedy was part of a predestined master plan, whether we like it or not. Frequently, those who are already on the other side of life know what will happen on earth, and if they are not able to prevent it, they are at least ready to help those who are coming across make the transition as painlessly as possible under the circumstances.

To the people of Ireland, the Kennedys can do no

wrong. Both Kennedys are great heroes to almost all Irish-men—far more so than they are to Americans. Both these thoughts should be kept in mind as I report still another psychic experience concerning the death of Robert Kennedy.

A fifty-three-year-old secretary by the name of Margaret M. Smith of Chicago, Illinois, was watching the Robert Kennedy funeral on television. As his casket was being carried out of the church to the hearse, she noticed a row of men standing at either side of the casket with their backs to it. They were dressed in gray business suits, very plain, and wore gray hats. These men looked very solemn and kept their eyes cast down. To her they looked like natives of Ireland. In fact, the suits looked homespun. As the casket went past, one of the men in the line turned his head and looked at the casket. Miss Smith thought that a person in a guard of honor should not do that, for she had taken the man in the gray suit as part of an honor guard. Then it occurred to her that the two lines of men were a little hazy, in a lighter gray. But she took this to be due to the television set, although other figures were quite clear. Later she discussed the funeral with a friend of hers in another city who had also seen the same broadcast. She asked her friend if she knew who the men in gray had been. Her friend had not seen the men in gray, nor had any of the others she asked about them. Soon it became clear to Miss Smith that she alone had seen the spirit forms of what she takes to be the Kennedys' Irish ancestors, who had come to pay their last respects in a fitting manner.

An Indiana amateur prognosticator with a long record of predictions, some of which have already come true while others are yet in the future, has also contributed to the material about the Kennedys. On August 7, 1968, D. McClintic stated that Jackie Kennedy would be married. At the time no such event was in the offing. On September 21, 1968, Mr. McClintic stated that there would be an attempted kidnapping of one of the Kennedy boys. At the same time he also predicted that the heads of the FBI and the draft would be replaced within a short time. "J. E. Hoover is near the end of being director. Also the director of the draft, Hershey, is on the way out."

A different kind of prognosticator is Fredric Stoessel. A college graduate and former combat Naval officer, he heads his own business firm in New York, specializing in market analysis and financing. Mr. Stoessel is a student of Christian Science and has had psychic experiences all his life. I have written of his predictions concerning the future of the world in a book entitled *The Prophets Speak*. However, his involvement with the Kennedy family, especially the future of Ted Kennedy, is somewhat more elaborate than his predictions pertaining to other events. In May 1967 he wrote an article entitled, "Why Was President Kennedy Shot?" In Mr. Stoessel's opinion a Communist plot was involved. Mr. Stoessel bases his views on a mixture of logical deduction, evaluations of existing political realities, and a good measure of intuition and personal insight ranging all the way to sixth sense and psychic impressions.

"There is some growing evidence to indicate Senator Ted Kennedy may have been set up for this incident. By whom is not certain, but we suspect the fine hand of organized crime." Thus stated Fredric Stoessel in February 1970. I discussed this matter with him on April 3 of the same year at my home. Some of the things he told me were off the record and I must honor his request. Other details may be told here. Considering Fredric Stoessel's background and his very cautious approach when making statements of importance at a time the Chappaquiddick incident was still in the news, I felt that perhaps he might come up with angles not covered by anyone else before.

"What then is your intuitive feeling about Kennedy and the girl? Was it an accident?" I asked. I decided to use the term "intuitive" rather than "psychic," although that is what I really meant.

Mr. Stoessel thought this over for a moment. "I don't think it was an accident. I think it was staged, shall we say."

"What was meant to happen?"

"What was meant to happen was political embarrassment for Teddy Kennedy. They were just trying to knock him out as a political figure."

"Do you think that he was aware of what had happened —that the girl had drowned?"

"No, I do not. I think he was telling the truth when he said that he was in a state of shock."

"How did 'they' engineer the accident?"

"I assume that he may have been drinking, but frankly it's an assumption. I think they would just wait until they had the right setup. I'm sure a man like that was watched very carefully."

"Have you any feelings about Kennedy's future?"

"I think Ted Kennedy will make a very strong bid for the presidency in 1972. I do not think he will be elected."

"Do you have any instinctive feelings about any attack upon him?"

"I have had an instinctive feeling that there would be an

attack on Ted Kennedy from the civil rights elements. In other words, I think he would be attacked so that there would be a commotion over civil rights. Undoubtedly Ted Kennedy will be the civil rights candidate."

"When you say 'attack,' can you be more specific?"

"I think it will be an assassination attempt; specific, shot."

"Successful or not?"

"No, unsuccessful. This is instinctive."

"How much into the future will this happen?"

"I think it will happen by 1972. I'm not too sure exactly when, but I think when he is being built up for a candidate."

"As far as the other Kennedys were concerned, did you at any time have any visions, impressions, dreams, or other feelings concerning either the president or Bobby Kennedy?"

"Well, I had a very strong sensation—in fact I wrote several people—that he would not be on the ticket in 1964. I had a strong impression that John F. Kennedy would *not be around* for some reason or another."

"When did you write this?"

"That was written to Perkins Bass, who was a Congressman in New Hampshire, in 1962."

"Did you have any impressions concerning the true murderer of John F. Kennedy and the entire plot, if any?"

"As soon as the assassination occurred, in those three days when we were all glued to the television set, I was inwardly convinced that Oswald did not kill him. My impression of that was immediately reinforced, because Oswald was asking for an attorney named John Abt, who was a lawyer for the Communist Party. My instinctive feeling was that Castro had a lot to do with it."

"Prior to the killing of Robert Kennedy, did you have any inklings that this was going to happen?"

"My wife reminded me that I had always said Bobby would be assassinated. I said that for several months after John died."

"Do you believe there is a Kennedy curse in operation?"

"Yes. I think there are forces surrounding the Kennedy family that will bring tragedy to most every one of them."

"Will we have another Kennedy president?"

"I don't think so. Although I think Teddy will make a strong bid for it this next time."

How much of all this is fact, how much fantasy, only the future can tell. Certainly if a direct pipeline could be established to one of the Kennedys—those on the other side of life, that is—even more interesting material could be obtained. But to make such an attempt at communication requires two very definite things: one, a channel of communication—that is to say, a medium of the highest professional and ethical reputation—and two, the kind of questions that could establish, at least to the point of reasonable doubt, that communication really did occur between the investigator and the deceased.

June Havoc *and the Colonial Ghosts*

"June Havoc's got a ghost in her townhouse," Gail Benedict said gaily on the telephone. Gail is in public relations, and a devoted ghost-finder ever since I was able to rid her sister's apartment of a poltergeist.

The house in question is over a hundred years old, stashed away in what New Yorkers call "Hell's Kitchen," the old area between Ninth and Tenth Avenue in the Forties, close to the theatre district. Built on the corner of 44th Street and 9th Avenue, the house was in the possession of the Rodenberg family until a Mr. Payne bought it. He remodeled it carefully; with a great deal of respect for the old plans, he did nothing to change its quaint Victorian appearance, inside and out.

Then glamorous stage and television star June Havoc bought the house, and rented the upper floors to various tenants. She herself moved into the downstairs apartment, simply because no one else wanted it. It did not strike her as strange at the time that no tenant had ever renewed the lease on that floor-through downstairs apartment, but she now realizes why. It is all because of Hungry Lucy.

The morning after Gail's call, June Havoc telephoned me and a séance was arranged for Friday of that week. I immediately reached British medium Sybil Leek, but I gave no details. I merely invited her to help me get rid of a noisy ghost. For noise was what June Havoc complained about.

"It seems to be a series of *insistent* sounds," she said. "First, they were rather soft. I didn't really notice them three years ago. Then I had the architect who built that balcony in the back come in and asked him to investigate these sounds. He said there was nothing whatever the matter with the house. Then I had the plumber up, because I thought it was the steam pipes. He said it was not that either. Then I had the carpenter in, for it is a very old house, but he couldn't find any structural defects whatever."

"When do you hear these tapping noises?"

"At all times. Lately, they seem to be more insistent. More demanding. We refer to it as 'tap dancing,' for that is exactly what it sounds like."

The wooden floors were in such excellent state that Miss Havoc did not cover them with carpets. The yellow pine wood used for the floorboards cannot be replaced today.

June Havoc's maid has heard loud tapping in Miss Havoc's absence, and many of her actor friends have remarked on it.

"It is always in this area," June Havoc pointed out, "and seems to come from underneath the kitchen floor. It has become impossible to sleep a full night's sleep in this room."

The kitchen leads directly into the rear section of the floor-through, which is used as a bedroom. Consequently, any noise would disturb her sleep. Underneath Miss Havoc's apartment, there is still another floor-through, but the tenants have never reported anything unusual there, nor have the ones on the upper floors. Only Miss Havoc's place is noisy.

We now walked from the front parlor half of the apartment into the back half. Suddenly there was a loud tapping sound from underneath the floor, as if someone had shot off a machine gun. Catherine and I had been a bit early, and there were just the three of us.

"There, you see," June Havoc said. The ghost had greeted us in style.

I stepped forward at once.

"What do you want?" I demanded.

Immediately, the noise stopped.

While we were waiting for the other participants in the investigation to arrive, June Havoc pointed to the rear wall.

"It has been furred out," she explained. "That is to say, there was another wall against the wall, which made the room smaller. Why, no one knows."

Soon, *New York Post* columnist Earl Wilson and Mrs. Wilson, Gail Benedict, and Robert Winter-Berger, also a publicist, arrived; a girl from *Life,* notebook in hand, came too. A little later Sybil Leek swept into the room. There was a bit of casual conversation, in which nothing whatever was said about the ghost, and then we seated ourselves in the rear portion of the apartment. Sybil took the chair next to the spot where the noises always originated, June Havoc sat on her right, and I on her left. The lights

were very bright since we were filming the entire scene for
Miss Havoc's television show.

Soon enough, Sybil began to "go under."

"Hungry," Sybil mumbled faintly.

"Why are you hungry?" I asked.

"No food," the voice said.

The usually calm voice of Sybil Leek was panting in des-
peration now.

"I want some food, some food!" she cried.

I promised to help her and asked for her name.

"Don't cry, I will help you," I promised.

"Food . . . I want some food," the voice continued to
sob.

"Who are you?"

"Lucy Ryan."

"Do you live in this house?"

"No house here."

"How long have you been here?"

"A long time."

"What year is this?"

"1792."

"What do you do in this house?"

"No house . . . people . . . fields. . . ."

"Why then are you here? What is there here for you?"
The ghost snorted.

"Hm . . . men."

"Who brought you here?"

"Came . . . people sent us away . . . soldiers . . .
follow them . . . sent me away. . . ."

"What army? Which regiment?"

"Napier."

"How old are you?"

"Twenty."

"Where were you born?"

"Hawthorne . . . not very far away from here."

I was not sure whether she said "Hawthorne" or "Hawgton" or some similar name.

"What is your father's name?"

Silence.

"Your mother's name?"

Silence.

"Were you baptized?"

"Baptized?"

She didn't remember that either.

I explained that she had passed on. It did not matter.

"Stay here . . . until I get some food . . . meat . . . meat and corn. . . ."

"Have you tried to communicate with anyone in this house?"

"Nobody listens."

"How are you trying to make them listen?"

"I make a noise because I want food."

"Why do you stay in one area? Why don't you move around freely?"

"Can't. Can't go away. Too many people. Soldiers."

"Where are your parents?"

"Dead."

"What is your mother's name?"

"Mae."

"Her maiden name?"

"Don't know."

"Your father's first name?"

"Terry."

"Were any of your family in the army?"

Ironical laughter punctuated her next words.

"Only . . . me."

"Tell me the names of some of the officers in the army you knew."

"Alfred. . . . Wait."

"Any rank?"

"No rank."

"What regiment did you follow?"

"Just this . . . Alfred."

"And he left you?"

"Yes. I went with some other man, then I was hungry and I came here."

"Why here?"

"I was sent here."

"By whom?"

"They made me come. Picked me up. Man brought me here. Put me down on the ground."

"Did you die in this spot?"

"Die, die? I'm not dead. *I'm hungry.*"

I then asked her to join her parents, those who loved her, and to leave this spot. She refused. She wanted to walk by the river, she said. I suggested that she was now receiving food and could leave freely. After a while, the ghost slipped away peacefully, it seemed, and Sybil Leek returned to her own body, temporarily vacated so that Lucy could speak through its speech mechanism. As usual, Sybil remembered absolutely nothing of what went on when she was in deep trance. She was crying, but thought her mascara was the cause of it.

Suddenly, the ghost was back. The floorboards were reverberating with the staccato sound of an angry tap, loud, strong and demanding.

"What do you want?" I asked again, although I knew now what she wanted.

Sybil also extended a helping hand. But the sound had stopped as abruptly as it had begun.

A while later, we sat down again. Sybil reported feeling two presences.

"One is a girl, the other is a man. A man with a stick. Or a gun. The girl is stronger. She wants something."

Suddenly, Sybil pointed to the kitchen area.

"What happened in the corner?"

Nobody had told Sybil of the area in which the disturbances had always taken place.

"I feel her behind me now. A youngish girl, not very well dressed, Georgian period. I don't get the man too well."

At this point, a small wooden table with three legs, of Victorian origin, the gift of Gail Benedict, was brought into the room.

Within seconds after Sybil, June Havoc, and I had lightly placed our hands upon it, it started to move, seemingly of its own volition!

Rapidly, it began to tap out a word, using a kind of Morse code. While Earl Wilson was taking notes, we allowed the table to jump hither and yon, tapping out a message.

None of us touched the table top except lightly; there was no question of manipulating the table. The light was very bright, and our hands almost touched, so that any pressure by one of us would have been instantly noticed by the other two. This type of communication is slow, since the table runs through the entire alphabet until it reaches the desired letter, then the next letter, until an entire word has been spelled out.

"L-e-a-v-e," the communicator said, not exactly in a friendly mood.

Evidently she wanted the place to herself and thought *we* were the intruders.

I tried to get some more information about her. But instead of tapping out another word in an orderly fashion, the table became very excited, if that is the word for emotional tables, and practically leapt out of our hands. We were required to follow it to keep up the contact, as it careened wildly through the room. When I was speaking, it ran up toward me and practically crept onto my lap; when I wasn't speaking, it ran to someone else in the room. Eventually, it became so wild, at times entirely off the floor, that it slipped from our light touch and instantly, as the power was broken, rolled into a corner—just another little table without a spark of life of its own.

We repaired to the garden, a few steps down an iron staircase, in the rear of the house.

"Sybil, what do you feel down here?" I asked.

"I had a tremendous urge to come out here. I didn't know there was a garden. Underneath my feet almost is the cause of the disturbance."

We were standing at a spot adjacent to the basement wall and close to the center of the tapping disturbance we had heard.

"Someone may be buried here," Sybil remarked, pointing to a mound of earth underneath our feet. "It's a girl."

"Do you see the wire covering the area behind you?" June Havoc said. "I tried to plant seeds there, and the wire was to protect them—but somehow nothing, nothing will grow there."

"Plant something on this mound," Sybil suggested. "It may well pacify *her.*"

We returned to the upstairs apartment, and soon after broke up the "ghost hunting party," as columnist Sheila

Graham had called it, although she had not managed to attend it.

The next morning, I called June Havoc to see how things were. I knew from experience that the ghost would either be totally gone, or totally mad, but not as before.

Lucy, I was told, was rather mad. Twice as noisy, she still demanded her pound of flesh. I promised June Havoc that we'd return until the ghost was completely gone.

A few days passed. Things became a little quieter, as if Lucy were hesitatlng. Then something odd happened the next night. Instead of tapping from her accustomed corner area, Lucy moved away from it and tapped away from above June's bed. She had never been heard before from this spot.

I decided it was time to have a chat with Lucy again. Meanwhile, corroboration of the information we had obtained had come to us quickly. The morning after our first séance, Bob Winter-Berger called. He had been to the New York Public Library and checked on Napier, the officer named by the medium as being the man in charge of her soldier's regiment.

The *Dictionary of National Biography* contained the answer. Colonel George Napier, a British officer, had served on the staff of Governor Sir Henry Clinton. How exciting, I thought. The Clinton mansion occupied the very ground we were having the séance on. In fact, I had reported on a ghost at Clinton Court, two short blocks to the north, in *Ghost Hunter* and again in *Ghosts I've Met,* and as far as I knew, the place was still not entirely free of the uncanny, for reports continued to reach me of strange steps and doors opening by themselves.

Although the mansion itself no longer stands, the carriage house in the rear of it is now part of Clinton Court, a reconstructed apartment house on West 46th Street. How could Sybil Leek, but recently arrived from England, have known of these things?

Napier was indeed the man who had charge of a regiment on this very spot, and 1781–82 is given as the time when Napier's family contracted the dreaded yellow fever and died. Sir Henry Clinton forbade his aide to be in touch with them, and the colonel was shipped off to England, half-dead himself, while his wife and family passed away on the spot that later became Potter's Field.

A lot of Irish immigrants came to the New World in those years. Perhaps the Ryan girl was one of them, or her parents were. History unfortunately does not keep much of a record of camp followers.

On January 15, 1965, precisely at midnight, I placed Sybil Leek into deep trance in my apartment on Riverside Drive. In the past we had succeeded in contacting *former* ghosts once they had been pried loose in an initial séance in the haunted house itself. I had high hopes that Lucy would communicate and I wasn't disappointed.

"Tick, tock, tickety-tock, June's clock stops, June's clock stops," the entranced medium murmured, barely audibly.

"Tickety-tock, June's clock stops, tickety-tock . . ."

"Who are you?" I asked.

"Lucy."

"Lucy, what does this mean?"

"June's clock stops, June's clock stops, frightened June, frightened June," she repeated like a child reciting a poem.

"Why do you want to frighten June?"

"Go away."

"Why do you want her to go away?"

"People there . . . too much house . . . too much June . . . too many clocks . . . she sings, she dances, she makes a lot of noise . . . I'm hungry, I'm always hungry. You don't do a thing about it. . . ."

"Will you go away if I get you some food? Can we come to an agreement?"

"Why?"

"Because I want to help you, help June."

"Ah, same old story."

"You're not happy. Would you like to see Alfred again?"

"Yes . . . he's gone."

"Not very far. I'll get you together with Alfred if you will leave the house."

"Where would I go?"

"Alfred has a house of his own for you."

"Where?"

"Not very far."

"Frightened to go . . . don't know where to go . . . nobody likes me. She makes noises, I make noises. I don't like that clock."

"Where were you born, Lucy?"

"Larches by the Sea . . . Larchmont . . . by the Sea . . . people disturb me."

Again I asked her to go to join her Alfred, if she were to find happiness again. I suggested she call for him by name, which she did, hesitatingly at first, more desperately later.

"No . . . I can't go from here. He said he would come. He said *wait*. Wait . . . here. Wait. Alfred, why don't you come? Too many clocks. Time, time, time . . . noisy creature. Time, time . . . three o'clock."

"What happened at three o'clock?" I demanded.

"He said he'd come," the ghost replied. "I waited for him."

"Why at three o'clock in the middle of the night?"

"Why do you think? Couldn't get out. Locked in. Not allowed out at night. I'll wait. He'll come."

"Did you meet any of his friends?"

"Not many . . . what would *I* say?"

"What was Alfred's name?"

"Bailey . . . Alfred said wait, wait . . . I'll go away, he said. They'll never find me."

"Go to him with my love," I said, calmly repeating over and over the formula used in rescue circle operations to send the earthbound ghost across the threshold.

As I spoke, Lucy slipped away from us, not violently as she had come, but more or less resignedly.

I telephoned June Havoc to see what had happened that night between midnight and twelve-thirty. She had heard Lucy's tapping precisely then, but nothing more as the night passed—a quiet night for a change.

Was Lucy on her way to her Alfred?

We would know soon enough.

In the weeks that followed, I made periodic inquiries of June Havoc. Was the ghost still in evidence? Miss Havoc did not stay at her town house all the time, but on the nights when she did sleep in the house on 44th Street, she was able to observe that Lucy Ryan had changed considerably in personality—the ghost had been freed, yes, but had not yet been driven from the house. In fact, the terrible noise was now all over the house, although less frequent and less vehement—as if she were thinking things over!

I decided we had to finish the job as well as we could and another séance was arranged for late March 1965. Present—in addition to our hostess and chief sufferer— were my wife, Catherine, and myself; Emory Lewis, editor of *Cue* magazine; Barry Farber, WOR commentator; and two friends of June Havoc. We grouped ourselves around a table in the *front room* this time. This soon proved to be a mistake. No Lucy Ryan. No ghost. We repaired to the other room where the original manifestations had taken place. More luck this time.

Sybil, in trance, was able to bring on a ghost. No, not Lucy Ryan. It was Alfred this time, Lucy's boyfriend from Col. Napier's Regiment. The one who says, "wait!"

Sybil, in trance, told us that the girl had gone, but that Alfred had no intention of leaving. He was waiting for *her* now. I asked for the name of his commanding officer and was told it was Napier. This we knew already. But who was the next in rank?

"Lieutenant William Watkins."

"What about the commanding general?"

He did not know.

He was born in Hawthorne, just like Lucy, he told Sybil. I had been able to trace this Hawthorne, incidentally. It is a place not far away in Westchester County.

There were people all over, Sybil said in trance, and they were falling down. They were ill.

"Send Alfred to join his Lucy," I commanded, and Sybil in a low voice told the stubborn ghost to go.

After an interlude of table tipping, in which several characters from the nether world made their auditory appearance, she returned to trance. Sybil in trance was near the river again, among the sick.

But no Lucy Ryan. Lucy's gone, she said.

"The smell makes me sick," Sybil said, and you could see stark horror on her sensitive face.

"Dirty people, rags, people in uniform too, with dirty trousers. There is a big house across the river."

"Whose house is it?"

"Mr. Dawson's. Doctor Dawson, Dr. James Dawson . . . Lee Point. Must go there. Feel sick. Rocks and trees, just the house across the river."

"What year is this?"

"Ninety-two."

She then described Dr. Dawson's house as having three windows on the left, two on the right, and five above, and said that it was called Lee Point—Hawthorne. It sounded a little like Hawgton to me, but I can't be sure.

Over the river, she said. She described a "round thing on a post" in front of the house, like a shell. For messages, she thought.

"What is the name of the country we're in?" I asked.

"Vinelands. Vinelands."

I decided to change the subject back to Hungry Lucy. How did she get sick?

"She didn't get any food, and then she got cold, by the river.

". . . Nobody helped them here. Let them die. Buried them in a pit."

"What is the name of the river?"

"Mo . . . Mo-something."

"Do you see anyone else still around?"

"Lots of people with black faces, black shapes."

The plague, I thought, and how little the doctors could do in those days to stem it.

I asked about the man in charge and she said "Napier" and I wondered who would be left in command after Napier left, and the answer this time was, "Clinton . . . old fool. Georgie."

There were, of course, a Henry Clinton and a George Clinton, fairly contemporary with each other.

"What happened after that?"

"Napier died."

"Any other officers around?"

"Little Boy Richardson . . . Lieutenant."

"What regiment?"

"Burgoyne."

Sybil, entranced, started to hiss and whistle. "Signals," she murmured, "as the men go away, they whistle."

I decided the time had come to bring Sybil out of trance. She felt none the worse for it, and asked for something to drink. *Hungry,* like Lucy, she wasn't.

We began to evaluate the information just obtained. Dr. James Dawson may very well have lived. The A.M.A. membership directories aren't quite that old. I found the mention of Lee Point and Hawthorne interesting, inasmuch as the two locations are quite close. Lee, of course, would be Fort Lee, and there is a "point" or promontory in the river at that spot.

The town of Vinelands does exist in New Jersey, and the river beginning with Mo- may be the Mohawk. That Burgoyne was a general in the British army during the Revolution is, of course, well known.

So there you have it. Sybil Leek knows very little, if anything, about the New Jersey and Westchester countryside, having but recently come to America. Even I, a New York resident for twenty-seven years, had never heard of Hawthorne before. Yet, there it is, on the way to Pleasantville, New York.

The proof of the ghostly pudding, however, was not the regimental roster, but the state of affairs at June Havoc's house. A later report had it that Lucy, Alfred, or whoever it may have been who was responsible, had considerably quieted down.

They were down, but not out.

I tactfully explained to June Havoc that feeling sorry for a hungry ghost makes things tough for a ghost hunter. The emotional pull of a genuine attachment, no matter how unconscious it may be, can provide the energies necessary to prolong the stay of the ghost.

Gradually, as June Havoc—wanting a peaceful house, especially at three A.M.—allowed practical sense to outweigh sentimentality, the shades of Hungry Lucy and her soldier-boy have faded into the distant past, from whence they came.

Telly Savalas's *Favorite Ghost*

Comedian Red Buttons and his wife, Alicia, had a lovely old apartment on New York's Central Park West. They always stayed there when they were in Manhattan. The building, which is at least seventy years old, houses many artistic people. The dark corridors lead to spacious, high-ceilinged luxury apartments constructed in a style no longer possible today.

Both Red and Alicia were born under the progressive astrological sign Aquarius. Alicia has long known her powers of psychic healing and has shown a keen interest in parapsychology. Red, best known as a comedian, also has a healthy curiosity about the Unknown, and does not necessarily find it funny. The more so as he himself has had a brush with it.

On more than one occasion, the Buttons would return to their apartment, which they knew to be empty, only to discover that there was "someone" already there ahead of them. This strong feeling of a presence did not particularly upset them, but they wished they could also see who it was they were sharing their apartment with. Their wish was soon to be fulfilled. One evening, they again felt the presence, and as they looked in back of the sofa, there was the faint outline of a woman dressed in Victorian clothes!

They made inquiries as to who the stranger might be, but to no avail. Friends who have stayed at the apartment have also reported the ghostly lady, and though the Buttonses do not know her name, they have long since become accustomed to her face. They simply refer to her as "that Spanish lady" because of the mantilla she wears when she puts in an appearance.

Telly Savalas comes from Astoria, Queens, where ghosts are rare. Once he was on his way to the airport during a personal-appearance tour. Everything had been arranged and a lot of people were waiting for him at the other end of the journey. Suddenly his car came upon a man standing in the road. Telly, who was alone in his car, stopped abruptly so as not to run the stranger down. The man, who was wearing a white suit, motioned him to follow him off the road into the woods lining the highway. Without hesitation, Telly got out of his car and followed the stranger. When they were away a distance and assured of privacy, the man in the white suit asked Telly not to continue his journey to the airport, because the plane he was to take would surely crash. Again, without a moment's hesitation, Telly nodded and turned around to return to his car. When he looked again, the man in the white suit had disappeared from view. But it did not matter to the actor. He returned home without continuing his trip. A short time later, news reports spoke of a plane crash—the very plane he was supposed to have taken!

The reason Telly followed the stranger's advice so

quickly and without question is a very special one: he recognized the stranger's face. It was a fellow Greek, a famous athlete who had passed away some time before.

When actor Darren McGavin wasn't yet piloting riverboats or chasing nightstalkers, he was growing up in Connecticut, where he lived with a relative who happened to be a Spiritualist minister. Thus young Gavin was present whenever his aunt held séances to contact the dead, and he thought it was all a lot of nonsense at the time.

One particular night, however, Darren decided to watch the proceedings from a place in hiding, something he was not supposed to do. What Darren saw made him wonder how it was all done. For he saw objects in the séance room take off by themselves and sail through the air, and a trumpet floated in the semidarkened room with a deep voice speaking from it. Far from being afraid, Darren thought it all a lot of fun and admired the away his aunt was fooling those people who had come to the séance.

When everyone had left the room, Darren quickly entered to inspect the contraptions and apparatus to operate all those flying objects. To his utter consternation, he found none. No wires, no machines, no hooks that could have accounted for the levitation phenomena he had witnessed. Suddenly it dawned on him that the phenomena had been genuine, and a cold fear crept up his back. But he never laughed at psychic experiences again.

In the world of make-believe, the line between reality and fantasy is very thin indeed. The late actor Larry Blyden and his dancer wife, Carol Haney, had a wonderful old farmhouse in Bergen County, New Jersey, built in 1704. The only problem was that the original owner kept on appearing to them, until we held a séance and found out that all he wanted was flowers placed on the graves of his children "on the hillock behind the house." Sure enough, there we found a much-neglected grave and did the right thing: the haunting then stopped.

When actress Gloria DeHaven got into her car that night, the weather looked menacing but she decided to get going anyway, hoping the weather would hold until she got to her destination in the country.

By the time it was pitch dark, the clouds had turned into a heavy downpour. Bravely, Gloria carried on in her little car. At times she could not even see the road ahead of her. The cloudburst was accompanied by thunder and lightning, not making her journey any easier. But she had to keep going, she was expected and did not wish to disappoint her friends.

Suddenly there appeared at her windshield the face of her long-dead mother, looking at her in great alarm. The sight of her mother so startled Gloria that she immediately stopped the car. Then she noticed that her mother had raised her right hand in a gesture of warning. Immediately the car stopped, the vision disappeared. Gloria decided to take the opportunity to check on the road. When she got out of her car she realized why her late mother had come to warn her. Just inches ahead of her car, the road had been washed out completely. Had she continued for another minute, she would have been swept down an embankment to certain death!

Elizabeth Taylor's *Ghostly Premonition*

Many artistic people, especially actors and actresses, frequently have psychic experiences. Perhaps because they work with their emotions, perhaps because they are more in tune with the fine "vibrations" all around us that herald coming events—it is a fact that the percentage of ESP incidents is far greater among sensitive people in the arts and professions than the more earthy pursuits such as bricklayers and farmers.

At the time of the incident in question, Elizabeth Taylor was married to Broadway producer Michael Todd. Although Taylor, a Piscean by birth, had always had a deep interest in the occult and accepted the advantages of being "different" without questioning, she was nevertheless a rational person who did not allow the extra sense to become a crutch in her life either. One could hardly accuse her of being a "believer," and yet she knew from many small incidents in her life that there was something within her that allowed her to have premonitions that later came true. At first this had upset her somewhat, but later she began to realize that the gift she had within herself was actually a blessing in disguise—provided it was used wisely. Then, too, she was in no way responsible for what came "through" her, and she considered herself simply an instrument of a Higher Power in this respect.

Mike Todd, on the other hand, had no particular beliefs of any kind. His world was the hard world of glitter and the struggle for survival in a business perhaps more precarious than any other. Already he had made his mark with successful Broadway shows, and his "Star and Garter" show had been the highlight of the New York World's Fair. His career was now at its zenith and he looked forward to many more successful enterprises in films and on the Broadway stage. His marriage to Elizabeth Taylor, who had of course been married before, was in fact a very happy one. Though they were on a different level of consciousness, the bond between Todd and Taylor was indeed very strong. In any psychic experience, personal emotional bonds between "sender" and "receiver" play an important role. In this case, the tie between the two principals was a major factor in the uncanny event that was to follow shortly.

On one particular morning, Elizabeth Taylor rose with heavy forboding in her mind. Something terrible was about to happen and she did not know what, or to whom. She passed the day nervously and as evening came she still did not know what was the matter. Later the foreboding was so strong she could hardly sit still. Finally she *knew*. Urgent business in New York required Mike Todd's presence. He would take his small plane, as he had done before; back in a week.

Elizabeth Taylor implored her husband not to get on

that plane. He laughed it off. After he had left, the actress sat practically paralyzed waiting for what she knew was sure to come.

Bad weather en route had enveloped the small plane, which crashed with no survivors. Once again, to her agony, Elizabeth Taylor knew that her Second Sight had been accurate.

Elizabeth Taylor never forgot the incident and her inability to save her "nonbelieving" husband's life. Several years later, while I was working with the famed trance medium Ethel Johnson Meyers in New York, I was asked to arrange for an experimental séance at the home of actor Darren McGavin in Greenwich Village. I took great care not to tell Mrs. Meyers where we were going that night, nor who might be present, thus she really had no idea what was about to transpire shortly after we arrived and she had seated herself in a comfortable chair.

Present with us was of course the host and his wife, the actress Lee Grant, and a few others, including Eva Gabor, her husband, and a pleasant-looking, quiet young man whose name I failed to catch, who had come with them.

Before long, Ethel was in deep trance and her spirit guide came to begin the proceedings as was the custom. But then another personality manifested through the medium's vocal apparatus, changing the timbre of her voice abruptly to a husky male voice. Speaking to us, this entity expressed much sorrow at not having listened to his wife. At one point, the medium, now speaking with his voice and personality, leaned forward toward the young man and extended her hands toward him. The young man seemed visibly shaken and responded hesitatingly with a few words.

After the séance, I asked him what he felt about this particular communicator. It was only now that I realized that the young man was Michael Todd, Jr., and the communicator had been his late father. He recognized the voice and mannerisms immediately as authentic. There would have been no way in which the medium could have guessed the identity of this young man.

Elke Sommer's *Haunted Dream House*

When Elke Sommer and husband, Hollywood journalist Joe Hyams, moved into their new home a few years ago, they were hoping for some peace and quiet—after all, Elke's career left her very little of that. Instead, they soon found themselves the center of a violent struggle between unseen forces, forces that evidently did not want them in the house.

At first, they tried to ignore the strange goings on. Doors opening by themselves, noises of people walking around downstairs when they were in bed upstairs and knew the downstairs was empty, and strange smells kept them in a perpetual state of nervousness. Elke, born under the Zodiac sign Scorpio, is a natural psychic, and she felt the intrusion more strongly.

But things would not stay ignored. A short man with a black hat was seen in the driveway, only to fade into nothingness immediately after. A fire of unknown origin started by itself in part of the house and had it not been for their quick action, the house would have burned to cinders.

A photographer interested in psychic phenomena, working for *Life* magazine, came up with some very strange photographic evidence that something unusual was in residence at the house. But Elke and Joe liked their home and they wanted to get rid of whoever it was who was causing them all this.

Thus a succession of psychics and mediums began to come to the house, ranging from the sincerely reputable to the downright useless who came in search of publicity. They all reported ghosts in residence, though they differed in their descriptions. Still, it became clear to Elke and Joe that their dream house was, in fact, haunted.

In the end, they left the house and moved elsewhere. They were told the ghost had resented the changes they had made in the house, but Elke and Joe liked things their way and decided to let the next owner struggle with the headstrong ghost!

The Ghostly Presence *of* William Butler Yeats

All along the Irish countryside, whenever I got to talk about ghosts, someone mentioned the ghost at Renvyle. Finally, I began to wonder about it myself. In Dublin, I made inquiries about Renvyle and discovered that it was a place in the West of Ireland. Now a luxury hotel, the old mansion of Renvyle in Connemara was definitely a place worth visiting sometime, I thought. As luck would have it, the present manager of the Shelbourne in Dublin had worked there at one time.

I immediately requested an interview with Eoin Dillon, and that same afternoon I was ushered into the manager's office tucked away behind the second floor suites of the hotel.

Mr. Dillon proved to be an extremely friendly, matter-of-fact man, in his early middle years, impeccably dressed as is the wont of hotel executives.

"I went to Renvyle in 1952," he explained, "as manager of the hotel there. The hotel was owned originally by the Gogarty family, and St. John Gogarty, of course, was a famous literary figure. He had written a number of books; he was also the original Buck Mulligan in James Joyce's *Ulysses*, and he was a personal friend of every great literary figure of his period.

"The house itself was built by Sir Edward Lutchins about 1932, but it stood on the site of the original Gogarty house, which was burnt down in the Troubled Times, some say without any reference to critical facts."

What Mr. Dillon meant was that the I.R.A. really had no business burning down this particular mansion. More great houses were destroyed by the Irish rebels for reasons hardly worthy of arson than in ten centuries of warfare. Ownership by a Britisher, or alleged ownership by an absentee landlord, was enough for the partisans to destroy the property. It reminded me of the Thirty Years' War in Europe when mere adherence to the Catholic or Protestant faith by the owner was enough to have the house destroyed by the opposition.

"What happened after the fire?" I asked.

"The site being one of the most beautiful in Ireland, between the lake and the sea, the hotel was then built. This was in 1922. Following the rebuilding of the house, Gogarty, who ran it as a rather literary type of hotel, collected there a number of interesting people, among them the poet and Nobel prize winner W. B. Yeats, whose centenary we are celebrating this year. And Yeats, of course, was very interested in psychic phenomena of one kind or another and has written a number of plays and stories on the subject. He also went in for séances. We were told that some of the séances held at Renvyle were very successful.

"Now the background to the piece of information which I have is that during the years preceding my arrival it had been noted that one particular room in this hotel was causing quite a bit of bother. On one or two occasions people came down saying there was *somebody* in the room, and on one very particular occasion, a lady whom I knew as a sane and sensible person complained that a man was looking over her shoulder while she was making her face up at the mirror. This certainly caused some furor."

"I can imagine—watching a lady put on her 'face' is certainly an invasion of privacy—even for a ghost," I observed.

"Well," Mr. Dillon continued, "when I went there the hotel had been empty for about a year and a half. It had been taken over by a new company and I opened it for that new company. My wife and I found some very unpleasant sensations while we were there."

"What did you do?"

"Finally, we got the local parish priest to come up and do something about it."

"Did it help?"

"The entire house had this atmosphere about it. We had Mass said in the place, during which there was a violent thunderstorm. We somehow felt that the situation was under control. Around August of that particular year, my wife was ill and my father was staying in the hotel at the time. I moved to that particular room where the trouble had been. It is located in the center of the building facing into a courtyard. The house is actually built on three sides of a courtyard. It is one flight up. This was thirteen years ago now, in August of 1952."

"What happened to you in the haunted room, Mr. Dillon?" I asked.

"I went to sleep in this room," he replied, "and my father decided he would sleep in the room also. He is a particularly heavy sleeper, so nothing bothers him. But I was rather tired and I had worked terribly hard that day, and as I lay in bed I suddenly heard this loud, clicking noise going on right beside my ears as if someone wanted to get me up! I refused to go—I was too tired—so I said, 'Will you please go away, whoever you are?'—and I put my blanket over my head and went to sleep."

"What do you make of it?" I said.

"There is a strong tradition that this room is the very room in which Yeats carried out these séances, and for that reason there was left there as a legacy actually some being of some kind which is certainly not explainable by ordinary standards."

"Has anyone else had experiences there?"

"Not the finger clicking. I assume that was to get my attention. But the wife of a musician here in town, whom I know well, Molly Flynn—her husband is Eamon O'Gallcobhair, a well-known Irish musician—had the experience with the man looking over her shoulder. He was tall and dressed in dark clothes."

"Have more people slept in this room and had experiences?"

"Over the years, according to the staff, about ten different people have had this experience. None of them knew the reputation the house had as being haunted, incidentally."

The reports of an intruder dated back only to Yeats's presence in the house, but of course something might have been latently present, perhaps "held over" from the earlier structure, and merely awakened by the séances.

It was not until the following summer that our hopes to go to Renvyle House were realized. Originally we had asked our friend Dillon to get us rooms at this renowned resort hotel so we could combine research with a little loafing in the sun—but as fate would have it, by the time we were ready to name a date for our descent upon the Emerald Isle, every nook and cranny at Renvyle House had been taken. Moreover, we could not even blame our ever-present countrymen, for the American tourist, I am told, waits far too long to make his reservations. The Britisher, on the other hand, having been taught caution and prevision by a succession of unreliable governments, likes to "book rooms," as they say, early in the season, and consequently we found that Connemara was once again British—for the summer, anyway.

We were given the choice of bedding down at nearby Leenane where Lord ffrench is the manager of a rather modern hotel built directly upon the rocky Connemara soil on the shore of a lough several miles deep. These loughs, or fjords, as they are called in Norway, are remnants of the ice ages, and not recommended for swimming, but excellent for fishing, since the Connemara fish apparently don't mind the cold.

Connemara is the name of an ancient kingdom in the westernmost part of Ireland, which was last—and least—in accepting English custom and language, and so here in the cottages along the loughs and the magnificent Connemara seacoast you can hear the softly melodic tongue of old Erin still spoken as a natural means of expression. This, of course, is a far cry from the politically inspired "Gaelization" of Irish public life, which is not likely to succeed since Gaelic is impractical for modern business relations, no matter how pretty it sounds. Any language that spells Owen "Eoin," O'Gonahue "O'Gallcobhair," and Dunleary "Dun Laoghaire," is not likely to be practical. But the Irish need not worry about speaking English, a foreign

tongue: the way many of them speak it, you would never
know it is the same language. The lilting brogue and the
strange construction of sentences is as different from what
you can hear across the Straits as day and night. There is,
of course, a small percentage of literary and upper-class
Irishmen, especially in Dublin, whose English is so fine it
outshines that spoken in Albion, and that, too, is a kind of
moral victory over the English.

But we have left Lord ffrench waiting for our arrival at
the Hotel Leenane, and await us he did, a charming, mid-
dle-thirtyish man wild about fishing and genially aware of
the lure the area has for tourists. Leenane was pleasant and
the air was fresh and clear, around 65 degrees at a time
when New York was having a comfortable 98 in the shade.
My only complaint about the hotel concerned the walls,
which had the thickness of wallpaper.

The weather this month of July 1966 was exceptionally
fine and had been so for weeks, with a strong sun shining
down on our heads as we set out for Renvyle after lunch.
The manager, Paul Hughes, had offered to come and
fetch us in his car, and turned out to be far younger than I
had thought. At twenty-seven, he was running a major
hotel and running it well. It took us about three-quarters
of an hour, over winding roads cut through the ever-present Connemara rock, to reach the coastal area where
Renvyle House stands on a spot just about as close to
America—except for the Atlantic—as any land in the area
could be. The sea was fondling the very shores of the land
on which stood the white two-story house, and cows and
donkeys were everywhere around it, giving the entire
scene a bucolic touch. Mr. Hughes left us alone for a while
to take the sun in the almost tropical garden. After lunch I
managed to corner him in the bar. The conversation, in

Sybil Leek's presence, had avoided all references to ghosts, of course. But now Sybil was outside, looking over the souvenir shop, and Hughes and I could get down to the heart of the matter.

Mr. Hughes explained that the hotel had been rebuilt in 1930 over an older house originally owned by the Blakes, one of the Galway tribes, who eventually sold it to Oliver St. John Gogarty. I nodded politely, as Mr. Dillon had already traced the history of the house for me last summer.

"He was a doctor in Dublin," Hughes explained, "and he came here weekends and entertained people such as Joyce and Yeats and Augustus John."

Thank goodness, I thought, they did not have autograph hounds in Connemara!

Mr. Hughes had been the manager for three years, he explained.

"Ever notice anything unusual about any of the rooms?" I prodded.

"No, I haven't, although many of the staff have reported strange happenings. It seems that one of the maids, Rose Coine, saw a man in one of the corridors upstairs—a man who disappeared into thin air."

Miss Coine, it developed, was middle-aged, and rather shy. This was her week off, and though we tried to coax her later, at her own cottage, to talk about her experiences, she refused.

"She has experienced it a few times," Mr. Hughes continued. "I don't know how many, though."

"Has anyone else had unusual impressions anywhere in the hotel?"

"They say since the hotel was rebuilt it isn't as strong anymore."

"But didn't Miss Coine have her experience *after* the fire?"

"Yes," the manager admitted, "last year."

I decided to pay the haunted room, number 27, a visit. This was the room mentioned by Eoin Dillon in which he had encountered the ghostly manifestations. We ascended the wooden staircase, with Sybil joining us—my wife and I, and Mr. Hughes, who had to make sure the guests of number 27 were outside for the moment. The room we entered on the second floor was a typical vacation-time hotel room, fairly modern and impersonal in decor, except for a red fireplace in the center of the left wall. I later learned that the two rooms now numbered 27 and 18 were originally one larger room. I took some photographs and let Sybil gather impressions. Hughes quickly closed the outside door to make sure nobody would disturb us. Sybil sat down in the chair before the fireplace. The windows gave onto the courtyard.

"I have the feeling of something overlapping in time," Sybil Leek began. Of course, she had no idea of the "two Renvyles" and the rebuilding of the earlier house.

"I have a peculiar feeling around my neck," she continued, "painful feeling, which has some connection with this particular room, for I did not feel it a moment ago downstairs."

"Do you feel a presence here?" I asked directly.

"Yes," Sybil replied at once, "something . . . connected with pain. I feel as if my neck's broken."

I took some more pictures; then I heard Sybil murmur "1928." I immediately questioned her about the significance of this date. She felt someone suffered in the room we were in at that time. Also, the size of the room had been changed since.

"There is a presence in this area," she finally said with resolution. "A noisy presence. This person is rough."

After Sybil remarked that it might be difficult to get the fireplace going, we went to the adjoining room to see if the impressions there might be stronger.

"What do you sense here?" I asked.

"Fear."

"Can it communicate?"

"It is not the usual thing we have . . . just pain, strong pain."

"Someone who expired here?"

"Yes, but did not finish completely."

"Is the person here now?"

"Not the person, but an impression."

"How far back?"

"I only get as far back as 1928."

I questioned Paul Hughes. That was indeed the time of the Yeats séances.

"What sort of people do you feel connected with this room?"

"There is this overlapping period . . . 1928 I feel very vital, but beyond that we go down in layers . . . traveling people, come here, do not live here . . . does the word 'off-lander' mean anything?"

It did not to me.

"We're in 1928 now. Men in long dresses . . . religious, perhaps . . . men in long clothes? A group of men, no women. Perhaps ten men. Long coats. Sitting in front of a big fire."

"The one you feel hung up in the atmosphere here—is he of the same period?"

"No," Sybil replied, "this is of a later period."

"How did he get here?"

"This is someone who was living here . . . died in this room . . . fire . . . the people in the long clothes are earlier, can't tell if they're men or women, could be monks, too . . . but the one whom I feel in the atmosphere of this room, he is from 1928."

We left the room and walked out into the corridor, the same corridor connecting the area in which we had just been with number 2, farther back in the hotel. It was here that the ghost had been observed by the maid, I later learned. Sybil mentioned that there were ten people with long clothes, but she could not get more.

"Only like a photograph," she insisted.

We proceeded to the lovely library, which is adorned with wooden paneling and two rather large paintings of Saints Brigid and Patrick—and I noticed that St. Brigid wore the long, robelike dress of the ancient Gaelic women, a dress, incidentally, that some of Ireland's nineteenth-century poets imitated for romantic reasons. It reminded Sybil of what she had felt in the room upstairs.

From her own knowledge, she recalled that William Butler Yeats had a lady friend fond of wearing such ancient attire. Farfetched though this sounded, on recollection I am not so sure. We left the house, and Paul Hughes drove us up a mountain road to the cottage in which the maid who had seen the ghost lived.

Hughes would go in first and try and persuade her to talk to me. Should he fail, he would then get the story once more from her and retell it to us afresh. We waited about fifteen minutes in his car while the manager tried his native charm on the frightened servant woman. He emerged and shook his head. But he had at least succeeded in having her tell of her experiences to him once more.

"About a year ago," Hughes began, "in the ground floor corridor leading to room number 2, Mrs. Coine saw a man come through the glass door and go into room 2."

"What did she do?" I interrupted.

"It suddenly struck Miss Coine that there was nobody staying in room 2 at the time. So she went down into room 2 and could not see anybody! She suddenly felt weak, and the housekeeper was coming along wondering what had happened to her. But she would not talk about it at first for she thought it would be bad for business at the hotel."

"Ridiculous," I said. "American tourists adore ghosts."

"Well," Hughes continued, "earlier this year—1966—there was a lady staying in room 2. Her daughter was in room 38. After two nights, she insisted on leaving room 2 and was happy to take a far inferior room instead. There were no complaints after she had made this change."

I discovered that rooms 2 and 27 were in distant parts of the hotel, just about as far apart as they could be.

There was a moment of silence as we sat in the car and I thought it all over.

"Did she say what the man looked like that she saw?" I finally asked, referring to Miss Coine's ghost.

"Yes," Hughes replied and nodded serenely. "*A tall man*, a very tall man."

"And a flesh-and-blood man could not have left the room by other means?"

"Impossible. At that stage the new windows had not yet been put in and the windows were inoperable with the exception of a small fan window. This happened about lunchtime, after Mass, on Sunday. In 1965."

"And the strange behavior of the lady?"

"Between Easter and Whitsun, this year, 1966."

We walked back into the main lobby of the hotel. There, among other memorabilia, were the framed pictures of great Irish minds connected with Renvyle House.

Among them, of course, was one of William Butler Yeats.

I looked at it, long and carefully. Yeats was *a tall man*, a very tall man. . . .

In the winter of 1952–53, Oliver St. John Gogarty wrote a brief article for *Tomorrow* magazine entitled "Yeats and the Ghost of Renvyle Castle."

To begin with, the term *castle* was applied by *Tomorrow*'s editors, since Gogarty knew better than to call Renvyle House a castle. There *is* a Renvyle castle all right, and it still stands about two miles south of the hotel, a charred ruin of medieval masonry, once the property of the celebrated Irish pirate queen Grania O'Malley.

Gogarty's report goes back to the house that stood there prior to the fire. Our visit was to the new house, built upon its ruins. The popular tale of séances held at the Renvyle House must refer to the earlier structure, as none were held in the present one, as far as I know.

Gogarty's report tells of Yeats and his own interest in the occult; of one particular time when Mrs. Yeats, who was a medium, told of seeing a ghostly face at her window; of a séance held in an upstairs room in which the restless spirit of a young boy manifested who had died by his own hand there. Morgan Even, a Welshman who apparently was also a trance medium, was among the guests at the time, and he experienced an encounter with the ghost that left him frightened and weak.

"I felt a strange sensation. A feeling that I was all keyed up just like the tension in a nightmare, and with that terror that nightmares have. Presently, I saw a boy, stiffly upright, in brown velvet with some sort of shirt showing at his waist. He was about twelve. Behind the chair he stood, all white-faced, hardly touching the floor. It seemed that if he came nearer some awful calamity would happen to me. I was just as tensed up as he was—nightmare terrors, tingling air; but what made it awful was my being wide awake. The figure in the brown velvet only looked at me, but the atmosphere in the room vibrated. I don't know what else happened. I saw his large eyes, I saw the ruffles on his wrists. He stood vibrating. His luminous eyes reproved. He looked deeply into mine.

"The apparition lifted his hands to his neck and then, all of a sudden, his body was violently seized as if by invisible fiends and twisted into horrible contortions in midair. He was mad! I sympathized for a moment with his madness and felt myself at once in the electric tension of Hell. Suicide! Suicide! Oh, my God, he committed suicide in this very house."

As it transpired, the ghost had communicated with Yeats through automatic writing. He objected to the presence of strangers in his house. But Yeats responded to his objection with a list of commands of his own such as the ghost could hardly have expected. First, he must desist from frightening the children in their early sleep. He must cease to moan about the chimneys. He must walk the house no more. He must not move furniture or terrify those who sleep nearby. And, finally, he was ordered to name himself to Yeats. And this he did.

How could Yeats, a visitor, have known that the children at times used to rush down crying from their bedroom? Nor could he have guessed that it was the custom of the Blake family to call their sons after the Heptarchy.

And yet he found out the ghost's particular name. A name Gogarty had never gleaned from the local people though he lived for years among them.

The troubled spirit had promised to appear in the ghost room to Mrs. Yeats, as he was before he went mad sixty years before.

Presently, Mrs. Yeats appeared carrying a lighted candle. She extinguished it and nodded to her husband. "Yes, it is just as you said."

"My wife saw a pale-faced, red-haired boy of about fourteen years of age standing in the middle of the north room. She was by the fireplace when he first took shape. He had the solemn pallor of a tragedy beyond the endurance of a child. He resents the presence of strangers in the home of his ancestors. He is Harold Blake."

And now it became clear to me what Sybil Leek had felt. Upstairs, in the room nearly on the same spot where the ghostly boy had appeared in the *old* house, she had suddenly felt a terrible discomfort in her neck—just as the psychic Welshman had, all those years ago! Was she reliving the tragedy or was the pale boy still about?

But the maid had seen a tall stranger, not a young boy, and not in the haunted room, but far from it. Yeats had been terribly attached to this house, and, being a man of great inquisitiveness, was just the type to stay on even after death, if only to talk to the melancholy boy from his own side of the Veil!

Apparently, my account of these events inspired a journalist named Dianne Donovan, literary editor of a large Chicago daily, to follow in my footsteps and visit at Renvyle.

Handed my book *The Lively Ghosts of Ireland* by the

hotel manager, she then ensconced herself in the haunted room and lit a fire. But the ghost did not visit with her. "I don't read ghost stories as a rule, being a nonbeliever," she observed, but she does read them when they can be quoted liberally for a good story of her own. As for the ghostly Mr. Yeats, he probably didn't want to be quoted without permission, either . . . so he stayed away.

Encountering Robert Louis Stevenson

Helen Lillie Marwick is a newspaperwoman and writer who lives with her science-writer husband Charles in a delightful old house in Georgetown, Washington, D.C. It was on her insistence that I decided to pay a visit to the house once owned by Robert Louis Stevenson in Heriot Row, Edinburgh.

"A delightful Irish girl, Mrs. John Macfie, has bought the old Robert Louis Stevenson house and reports that the friendly ghost of R.L.S. himself has been around, and she hopes to keep him," Helen wrote.

I asked my friend Alanna to arrange for a visit during my stay in Edinburgh, and on May 4, 1973, she and I arrived at the Stevenson House barely in time for tea. We had been asked for five o'clock, but our adventures in the countryside had caused us to be an hour late. It wasn't so much the countryside as the enormous downpour that had accompanied this particular ghost hunt, and though it gave it a certain aura, it created havoc with our schedule. But Kathleen Macfie shook hands with us as if we were old friends and led us into the high-ceilinged drawing room, one flight up. The large French windows allowed us to look out on what is probably one of the finest streets in Edinburgh, and I could see at a glance that Mrs. Macfie had refurbished the Stevenson House in a manner that would have made Stevenson feel right at home: a gentle blend of Victorian and earlier furniture and casual displays of artwork in the manner of a home rather than a museum. Her own strong vibrations, as the owner, filled the place with an electrifying atmosphere of the kind that is so very conducive to psychic occurrences. Our hostess had blue eyes, red hair, and a direct practical approach to everything, including ghosts. After we had had a glass of sherry, she gave us the grand tour of the house. It had been the home of Robert Louis Stevenson from 1857 to 1880.

"This was Mrs. Stevenson's domain," our hostess explained. The magnificently furnished drawing room was pretty much the way it must have been in Stevenson's day, except for the addition of electric light and some of the personal belongings of the Macfies. In particular, there was a chair by the window that Stevenson is said to have sat in when resting from his work. As we walked in, I felt a distinct chill down my back, and I knew it wasn't due to the weather. It was a definite touch of some sort. I asked Alanna whether she had felt anything. She confirmed that she too had been touched by unseen hands, *a very gentle kind of touch*. "I feel a presence. There is definitely someone here other than ourselves." I turned to Mrs. Macfie. "What exactly have you felt since you came to this house?"

"I am most sensitive to a feeling when I am alone in the house, but maybe that isn't right, because I never feel alone here. There is always somebody or something here, a friendly feeling. Actually, there are two people here. At first I thought, perhaps because of what I had read about Robert Louis Stevenson, I was imagining things. But then the Irish writer James Pope Hennessey came to stay with us. Mr. Hennessey had been to Vailina, on Samoa, where Robert Louis Stevenson lived and ended his days. There, in the South Seas, he had seen an apparition of Stevenson, and in this house he had seen it also. It happened in his own room because he slept back there in what we called the master bedroom."

"Have *you* seen anything?"

"No, but I feel it all the time. It is as though I would look around and there was somebody behind me. Sometimes, when I wake up early in the morning, especially in the winter, I feel as if there is somebody moving about. It is very difficult to talk about it. You see, my husband is an utter skeptic. He thinks it is the central heating. Even my small son would say, 'Oh, don't listen to Mother. She sees ghosts everywhere.' You see, the family doesn't support me at all."

Kathleen Macfie admits to having had similar "feelings" in other houses where she has lived. When she arrived at the Stevenson House eighteen months prior to our conversation, she soon realized that it was happening again.

"While the movers were still bringing the stuff in, I didn't pay any attention to what I felt or heard. I thought it was just the noise the movers were making. But then the feeling came: you know, when you are looking in a certain way you have peripheral vision and feelings; you don't have to look straight at anything to see it. You know that it is there. But it is a comforting, marvelous feeling."

Some of the poet's personal belongings were still in the

house, intermingled with period pieces carefully chosen by the Macfies when they bought the house. "There is an invitation he sent to his father's funeral, with his own signature on it," Mrs. Macfie commented. "But when his father died, his mother took nearly all the furniture out of here and went to live in Samoa with her son. When Stevenson himself died, the mother came back to Edinburgh to live with her sister, but Robert Louis Stevenson's widow brought all the furniture back to St. Helena, California, where she ended her days. By the way, this is his parents' room. His own room is up one flight. Originally the top story was only half a story, and it was for the servants, but Stevenson's parents wanted him to have proper accommodations up there, so that he could study and work. The house was built between 1790 and 1810. The Stevensons bought it from the original builders, because they wanted a house on drier ground."

Mrs. Macfie explained that she was in the process of turning part of the house into a private museum, so that people could pay homage to the place where Robert Louis Stevenson lived and did so much of his work.

We walked up to the second floor, Stevenson's own study. The room was filled with bookcases, and next to it was a bedroom, which Mr. Macfie uses as a dressing room. Nowadays there is a bed in the study, but in Stevenson's time there was no bed; just a large desk, a coal scuttle, and of course lots of books. I turned to Alanna and asked if she received any impressions from the room. She nodded.

"Near the fireplace I get an impression of *him*. When I just came in through the door it was as if somebody were there, standing beside the door."

While she was speaking, it seemed to me as if I, too, were being shown some sort of vague scene, something that sprang to my mind unexpectedly and most certainly not from my own unconscious. Rather than suppress it or attribute it to our discussion of Robert Louis Stevenson, of whom I knew very little at that point, I decided to "let it rip," saying whatever I felt and seeing if it could be sorted out to make some sense.

"Is there a person connected with this house wearing a rather dark coat and a light-colored or white shirtwaist type of thing with a small tie? He has rather dark eyes and his hair is brushed down. He has bushy eyebrows and he seems rather pale and agitated, and at this moment he is tearing up a letter."

Miss Macfie seemed amazed. "Yes, that is him exactly. His desk used to be where you're standing, and this was where his mother used to leave food for him on a little stool outside. She would come back hours later and it would still be there."

"I get something about age thirty-four," I said.

"Well, he was married then. On May 9, 1880, in fact." This was May 4, almost an anniversary.

We stepped into the adjacent room, which was once Stevenson's bedroom. I asked Alanna whether she felt anything special. "The presence is much stronger here than in the other room," she said. Even while she was talking, I again had the strange urge to speak about something I knew nothing about.

"I have the impression of someone being desperately ill from a high fever and very lonely and near death. He's writing a letter to someone. He expects to die but survives nevertheless."

Both ladies nodded simultaneously. "During his teenage period, he was always desperately ill and never expected to survive," Alanna commented. "It was consumption, which today is called tuberculosis, an inflammation of the lungs."

Alanna Knight was eminently familiar with Robert Louis Stevenson, as she was working on a play about him. My knowledge of the great writer was confined to being aware of his name and what he had written, but I had not known anything about Stevenson's private life when I entered the house. Thus I allowed my own impressions to take the foreground, even though Alanna was far more qualified to delve into the psychic layer of the house.

"Was there any kind of religious conflict, a feeling of wanting to make up one's mind one way or the other? Is there any explanation of the feeling I had for his holding a crucifix and putting it down again, of being desperate, of going to consult with someone, of coming back and not knowing which way to turn?" I asked.

"This is absolutely accurate," Mrs. Macfie confirmed, "because he had a tremendous revulsion from the faith he had been brought up in, and this caused trouble with his father. He was Presbyterian, but he toyed with atheism and the theories of the early German philosophers. All of this created a terrible furor with his father."

"Another thing just went through my mind: was he at any time interested in becoming a doctor, or was there a doctor in the family?"

"He was trained as a lawyer, very reluctantly," Mrs. Macfie replied; "his father wanted him to become an engineer. But because of his uncertain health he never practiced law. His uncle, Dr. Louis Balfour, insisted that he leave Edinburgh for his health. His wife, Fannie Osborne, was very interested in medicine; she helped keep him alive."

Alanna seemed puzzled by something she "received" at

this moment. "Was there a dog of a very special breed, a very elegant dog? When he died, was there great upheaval because of it? I feel that there was a very strong attachment to this dog." Mrs. Macfie beamed at this. "There was a West Highland terrier that he took all over. The dog's name was Rogue and he was very attached to it."

We thanked our hostess and prepared to leave the house. It was almost dinnertime and the rain outside had stopped. As we opened the heavy door to walk out into Heriot Row, I looked back at Kathleen Macfie, standing on the first-floor landing smiling at us. Her husband had just returned and after a polite introduction excused himself to go upstairs to his room—formerly Robert Louis Stevenson's study and bedroom. Except for him and for Mrs. Macfie on the first-floor landing, the house was empty at this moment. Or was it? I looked back into the hallway and had the distinct impression of a dark-eyed man standing there, looking at us with curiosity, not sure whether he should come forward or stay in the shadows. But it probably was only my imagination.

Abraham Lincoln's *Terrible Secret*

I don't think anyone has had more trouble getting into the White House for a specific purpose than I except, perhaps, some presidential aspirants such as Thomas E. Dewey. But Mr. Dewey's purpose was a lot easier to explain than mine. How do you tell an official at the presidential mansion that you would like to go to the Lincoln Bedroom to see whether Lincoln's ghost is still there? How do you make it plain that you're not looking for sensationalism, that you're not bringing along a whole covey of newspaper people, all of which can only lead to unfavorable publicity for the inhabitants of the White House, whoever they may be at the time?

Naturally, this was the very difficult task to which I had put myself several years ago. Originally, when I was collecting material for *Window to the Past*, I had envisioned myself going to the Lincoln Bedroom and possibly the East Room in the White House, hoping to verify and authenticate apparitions that had occurred to a number of people in those areas. But all my repeated requests for permission to visit the White House in the company of a reputable psychic were turned down. Even when I promised to submit my findings and the writings based on those findings to White House scrutiny prior to publication, I was told that my request could not be granted.

The first reason given was that it was not convenient because the president and his family were in. Then it was not convenient because they would be away. Once I was turned down because my visit could not be cleared sufficiently with Security, and anyway, that part of the White House I wanted to visit was private.

I never gave up. Deep down I had the feeling that the White House belongs to the people and is not a piece of real estate on which even the presidential family may hang out a "No Trespassers" sign. I still think so. However, I got nowhere as long as the Johnsons were in the White House.

I tried again when I started work on this book. A colonel stationed in the White House, whom I met through a mutual friend, Countess Gertrude d'Amecourt, tried hard to get permission for me to come and investigate. He too failed.

Next, I received a letter, quite unexpectedly, from the Reverend Thomas W. Dettman of Niagara, Wisconsin. He knew a number of very prominent men in the federal government and offered to get me the permission I needed. These men, he explained, had handled government investigations for him before, and he was sure they would be happy to be of assistance if he asked them. He was even sure they would carry a lot of weight with the president. They knew him well, he asserted. Mr. Dettman had been associated with the Wisconsin Nixon for President Committee, and offered to help in any way he could.

After thanking Mr. Dettman for his offer, I heard nothing further for a time. Then he wrote me again explaining that he had as yet not been able to get me into the Lincoln Bedroom, but that he was still working on it. He had asked the help of Representative John Byrnes of Wisconsin in the matter, and I would hear further about it. Then Mr. Dettman informed me that he had managed to arrange for me to be given "a special tour" of the White House, and, to the best of his knowledge, that included the East Room. He then asked that I contact William E. Timmons, Assistant to the President, for details.

I was, of course, elated. Imagine, a special tour of the White House! What could be better than that?

With his letter, Mr. Dettman had included a letter from Senator William Proxmire of Wisconsin, in which the Senator noted that I would not be able to do research in the Lincoln Bedroom, but that I would be given the special tour of the White House.

I hurriedly wrote a thank-you note to Mr. Dettman, and started to make plans to bring a medium to Washington with me. A few days later Mr. Dettman wrote me again.

He had received a call from the White House concerning the tour. He could, he explained, in no way guarantee what *kind* of tour I would be given, nor what I would see. He had done everything possible to help me and hoped I would not be disappointed.

Whether my own sixth sense was working or not, I suddenly thought I had better look into the nature of that "special tour" myself. I wrote and asked whether I would be permitted to spend half an hour in the East Room, since the Lincoln Bedroom had been denied me. Back came a letter dated May 14, 1970, on White House stationery, and signed by John S. Davies, Special Assistant to the President, Office White House Visitors.

"Senator Proxmire's recent letter to Mr. William Timmons concerning your most recent request to visit the White House has been referred to me, as this office is responsible for White House visitors. Unfortunately, as we have pointed out, we are unable to arrange for you to visit the Lincoln Bedroom, as this room is in the President's personal residence area, which is not open to visitors. If you wish to arrange an early-morning special tour, I suggest you contact Senator Proxmire's office. You are also most welcome to come to the White House any time during the regular visiting hours."

I decided to telephone Mr. Davies since the day of my planned visit was close at hand. It was only then that I realized what that famous "special tour" really was. It meant that I, along with whoever else might be present at the time at the White House gates, would be permitted to walk through the part of the White House open to all visitors. I couldn't bring a tape recorder. I could not sit down or tarry along the way. I had to follow along with the group, glance up at whatever might be interesting, and be on my way again like a good little citizen. What, then, was so special about that tour, I inquired? Nothing really, I was told, but that is what it is known as. It is called a special tour because you have to have the request of either a senator or a representative from your home state.

I canceled my visit and dismissed the medium. But my reading public is large, and other offers to help me came my way.

Debbie Fitz is a teenage college student who wanted me to lecture at her school. In return, she offered to get me into the White House, or at least try to. I smiled at her courage, but told her to go right ahead and try. She wrote a letter to Miss Nixon, whom she thought would be favorable to her request, being of the same age group and all that. After explaining her own interest in ESP research and the importance this field has in this day and age for the young, she went on to explain who I was and that I had previously been denied admittance to the White House areas I wished to do research in. She wrote:

All he wants to do is take a psychic medium into the room and scientifically record any phenomena that may exist. This will not involve staying overnight; it can be done during the day at your convenience. All investigations are conducted in a scientific manner and are fully documented. It is well known that Lincoln himself was psychic and held séances in the White House. Wouldn't you, as a student of White House history and a member of the young, open-minded generation, like to find out whether or not this room is really haunted? This will also provide an opportunity for young people who are interested in other things besides riots and demonstrations to benefit intellectually from Mr. Holzer's efforts.

Debbie Fitz never received a reply or an acknowledgment. I, of course, never heard about the matter again.

Try as I would, I was rebuffed. Just the same, interest in the haunted aspects of the nation's Executive Mansion remains at a high level. Several Washington newspapers carried stories featuring some of the psychic occurrences inside the White House, and whenever I appeared on

Washington television, I was invariably asked about the
ghosts at the White House. Perhaps the best account of
the psychic state of affairs at number 1600 Pennsylvania
Avenue was written by the *Washington Post* reporter Jac-
queline Lawrence.

The most troubled spirit of 1600 Pennsylvania Avenue
is Abraham Lincoln, who during his own lifetime
claimed to receive regular visits from his two dead sons,
Pat and Willie. After reporting the well-known premonitory dream in which Lincoln saw himself dead in a casket in the East Room, Miss Lawrence goes on to report
that Mrs. Franklin Delano Roosevelt's servant, Mary
Evan, had reported seeing Lincoln on the bed in the
northwest bedroom, pulling on his boots. Other servants said they had seen him lying quietly in his bed,
and still others vowed that he periodically stood at the
oval window over the main entrance of the White
House. Mrs. Roosevelt herself never saw Lincoln, but
she did admit that when working late she frequently felt
a ghostly sort of presence.

Amongst the visitors to the White House who had
experienced psychic occurrences was the late Queen
Wilhelmina of the Netherlands. Asleep in the Queen's
Bedroom, she heard someone knock at her door, got
up, opened it, and saw the ghost of President Lincoln
standing there looking at her. She fainted, and by the
time she had come to he was gone.

According to the legend, the spirit of Lincoln is especially troubled and restless on the eve of national calam-
ities such as war. Under the circumstances, one should
expect the shade of President Lincoln to be in around-
the-clock attendance these days and nights.

But Lincoln is not the only ghost at the White House. Household members of President Taft observed the ghost of Abigail Adams walking right through the closed doors of the East Room with her arms outstretched. And who knows what other specters reside in these ancient and troubled walls?

That all is not known about the White House may be seen from a dispatch of the *New York Daily News* dated November 25, 1969, concerning two new rooms unearthed at the White House. "Two hitherto unknown rooms, believed to date back to the time of Thomas Jefferson, have been unearthed in the White House a few yards away from the presidential swimming pool. The discovery was made as excavation continued on the larger work area for the White House press corps. The subterranean rooms, which White House curator James Ketchum described as storage or coal bins, were believed to be among the earliest built at the White House. Filled with dirt, they contained broken artifacts believed to date back to President Lincoln's administration."

When I discussed my difficulties in receiving permission for a White House investigation with prominent people in Washington, it was suggested to me that I turn my attention to Ford's Theater, or the Parker House—both places associated with the death of President Lincoln. I have not done so, for the simple reason that in my estimation the ghost of Lincoln is nowhere else to be found but where it mattered to him: in the White House. If there is a transitory impression left behind at Ford's Theater, where he was shot, or the Parker House, where he eventually died some hours later, it would only be an imprint from the past. I am sure that the surviving personality of President Lincoln is to a degree attached to the White House because of unfinished business. I do not think that this is unfinished business only of his own time. So much of it has never been finished to this very day, nor is the present administration in any way finishing it. To the contrary, if there ever was any reason for Lincoln to be disturbed, it is now. The Emancipation Proclamation, for which he stood and which was in a way the rebirth of our country, is still only in part reality. Lincoln's desire for peace is hardly met in these troubled times. I am sure that the disturbances at the White House have never ceased. During the Johnson administration, the president's daughter Lynda heard someone knock at her door, opened it, and found no one outside. Telephone calls have been put through to members of the presidential family, and there has been no one on the other end of the line. Moreover, on investigating, it was found that the White House operators had not rung the particular extension telephones.

It is very difficult to dismiss such occurrences as products of imagination, coincidence, or "settling of an old house." Everyone knows the difference between human footsteps caused by feet encased with boots or shoes, and the normal noises of an old house settling slowly and a little at a time on its foundation.